The Joy of Life
Your Guide to Finding More Joy in Your Daily Life

Ingrid Johansson

Copyright © 2015 by Ingrid Johansson (the Author). All Rights Reserved.

No part of this book may be reproduced or transmitted in any form or by any means, electronic or mechanical, including photocopying, recording, or by an information storage and retrieval system – or otherwise be copied for public or private use – other than for "fair use" as brief quotations embodied in articles and reviews – without prior written permission of the Author.

The Author of this book does not dispense medical advice or prescribe the use of any technique as a form of treatment for physical, emotional, or medical problems without the advice of a physician, either directly or indirectly. The intent of the Author is only to offer information of a general nature to help you in your quest for emotional and spiritual well-being. In the event you use any of the information in this book for yourself, the Author and the Publisher assume no responsibility for your actions.

If professional assistance is required, the services of a competent professional person should be sought. Neither the Publisher nor the Author shall be liable for damages arising herefrom. The fact that an organization or website is referred to in this work as a citation and/or potential resource of further information does not mean that the Author or the Publisher endorses the information the organization or website may provide or recommendations it may make. Further, readers should be aware that internet websites listed in this work may have changed or disappeared between when this work was written and when it is read.

Published in the United States of America.
Printed by Create/Space, An Amazon.com Company
Cover Design: Eija Kuusela, Finland

First Edition 2015

ISBN-13: 978-1515382270
ISBN-10: 1515382273

The Joy of Life
Your Guide to Finding More Joy in Your Daily Life

Table of Contents

INTRODUCTION 1
WHAT IS JOY OF LIFE? 5
    Results of a Survey on Joy of Life 6
    Conclusion 10
KEY 1: SELF-KNOWLEDGE 11
    Who Have I Become? 12
    Self-esteem and Self-confidence 16
    Who Would I Like to Be? 19
    Passions 22
    Meaning and Purpose 25
KEY 2: OPENNESS TO CHANGE 29
    Why Change? 29
    Limiting Beliefs 33
    Attitudes 38
    Values 45
    Fear and Courage 46
    Worrying 51
KEY 3: GRATITUDE 55
KEY 4: FORGIVENESS 67
    Forgiving Yourself 77
KEY 5: NO REGRETS 81
    Leaving Behind and Moving on 87
    Curiosity and Learning 89
    Hope 93
KEY 6: LAUGHTER, SMILES AND HUMOUR 97
    Laughter 97
    Smiles 101

Humour	103
KEY 7: GOOD RELATIONSHIPS	**109**
Ways to Enhance Good Relationships	110
Friendship and Kindness	113
Respect	115
Communication and Connection	118
Generosity	121
Your Best Friend	124
ACKNOWLEDGEMENTS	**127**
NOTES	**129**

INTRODUCTION

Joy does not exist in the world, it exists in us.
Benjamin Franklin

There is a tapestry embroidered by my mother hanging above my bed with the words "Joy is the purpose of our lives". The tapestry used to hang on the wall in my parents' home. It had probably been there for many years. I never paid much attention to it at that time. When my mother died in 2007, I really wanted to have the tapestry because it now had a meaning for me. That same year I had been diagnosed with lung cancer but survived. Only about 15 percent of people with that diagnosis survive for five years and I was one of them.

Why did I survive when most people don't? I have never been able to let go of that question. Was there a special meaning? What more is there for me to do in my life that is important and meaningful? How can I use this second chance of living?

It has been said that terrifying experiences, such as cancer, a heart attack, life threatening accidents, the horror of war, the death of a child, spouse or other close persons can profoundly change your values and view on life. You start appreciating things that you took for granted before and complain less about matters that are not very important.

Researchers[1] confirm that a person who has been diagnosed with cancer, a survivor, will often lead a fuller and more meaningful life, appreciate being alive and have a more optimistic outlook. They go "from black and white to full colour".

Here is a story by Rachel Naomi Remen. The author, who is a medical doctor, tells about a man who got cancer and how this changed his way of looking at life.

Eating the Cookie

One of my patients, a successful businessman, tells me that before his cancer he would become depressed unless things went a certain way. Happiness was "having the cookie." If you had the cookie, things were good. If you didn't have the cookie, life wasn't worth a damn.

Unfortunately, the cookie kept changing. Some of the times it was money, sometimes power, sometimes sex. At other times, it was the new car, the biggest contract, the most prestigious address. A year and a half after his diagnosis of prostate cancer he sits shaking his head ruefully. "It's like I stopped learning how to live after I was a kid. When I give my son a cookie, he is happy. If I take the cookie away or it breaks, he is unhappy. But he is two and a half and I am forty-three. It's taken me this long to understand that the cookie will never make me happy for long. The minute you have the cookie it starts to crumble or you start to worry about it crumbling or about someone trying to take it away from you.

You know, you have to give up a lot of things to take care of the cookie, to keep it from crumbling and be sure that no one takes it away from you. You may not even get a chance to eat it because you are so busy just trying not to lose it. Having the cookie is not what life is about."

My patient laughs and says cancer has changed him. For the first time he is happy. No matter if his business is doing well or not, no matter if he wins or loses at golf. "Two years ago, cancer asked me: 'Okay, what's important? What is really important?' Well, life is important. Life. Life any way you can have it. Life with the cookie. Life without the cookie. Happiness does not have anything to do with the cookie, it has to do with being alive. Before, who made the time?" He pauses thoughtfully. "Damn, I guess life is the cookie."

Rachel Naomi Remen[2]

That is what happened to me, too, after surviving lung cancer. I was so grateful for being alive. I had never before known how very much I wanted to live and now I felt very strongly that I did not want to waste that second chance of living by being negative, depressed, resentful, or ungrateful. I wanted to have a life full of joy and share that joy of life with other people.

If you have had a similar experience, I am sure you know what I am talking about. But isn't it ironic and sad that you have to experience something extremely bad or serious before you realize how important joy is and that you have a choice whether or not to have a life full of joy? Shouldn't that be obvious and self-evident to all of us irrespective of our experiences? With this book I hope to help you find more joy in your daily life and go from black and white to full colour, without first having a terrifying life threatening experience.

I believe that a shift in focus after a serious and life threatening disease or accident may also have to do with a shift in the time horizon. Laura L. Carstensen[3] describes how research has shown that older people, who have a shorter time horizon than younger people, have more positive emotional experiences than younger people with a more open-ended time horizon. Surviving a life-threatening situation makes you feel closer to death, irrespective of your age and your life horizon changes. Thus you start focusing more on positive experiences and feelings.

In my case this change in focus did not come overnight but grew slowly during the years after my disease. One of the things I realized was that I wanted to become a better person. The result was that I started to read a great deal about personal development. Although much of it was already familiar to me I also learnt many things that I did not know before or had just not thought of and began to view things in a new way.

My need to share my knowledge and experience, or wisdom, also grew. I wanted to contribute more. How can I help other people find joy in their lives? I took one significant step on that road when I decided to go to Arizona in the US to attend a course and become a certified facilitator of The Passion Test[4].

As a facilitator of The Passion Test, I had learnt a powerful method to help people obtain clarity about their passions, discover what they are burning for, what engages them most and how to choose to live aligned with their passions. Clarity is a key word of The Passion Test.

In order to work with clients I needed a company and I am now very proud of having a company called Senior Life Joy (www.seniorlifejoy.com). My intention was to have seniors as my main target group as I am a senior myself.

The name of my company made me think even more about the joy of life and its significance and meaning. What is the joy of life and how can we find more and lasting joy in our daily lives? That is what this book is about.

The transition from work to retirement may be an example of an opportunity to reflect on how to find lasting joy in the rest of your life. However, there are many other occasions in life that may especially motivate you to stop, reflect and make choices. Examples are when you lose your job, go through a divorce, your children move away from home or you yourself move to another city or country. What I am writing about in this book concerns everybody, both younger and older people.

I have identified seven keys to finding more joy of life. I do not presume to cover all possible keys but I will describe the ones I believe in and think will be valuable to you when you are searching for more joy of life. I do hope you will find the keys useful and I welcome your comments or questions on info@seniorlifejoy.com.

Here are the seven keys:

1. Self-knowledge
2. Openness to change
3. Gratitude
4. Forgiveness
5. No regrets
6. Laughter, smiles and humour
7. Good relationships

WHAT IS JOY OF LIFE?

Joy seems to me a step beyond happiness – happiness is a sort of atmosphere you can live in sometimes when you're lucky. Joy is a light that fills you with Hope, Faith and Love.
Adela Rogers St. Johns

Before you continue to read about the seven keys to joy of life I would like to discuss the concepts of happiness, joy and joy of life, as well as their possible significance.

I searched on the Internet, in books and in dictionaries and talked to many people without finding a unanimous answer. Sometimes I found that happiness has to be earned and is dependent on external objectives. On the other hand, there were also descriptions of happiness as coming from the inside and not related to external objectives.

I found descriptions of joy as being something "more" than happiness that is deeper and lasts for a longer time. Rachel Naomi Remen[1], who told the story about the cookie that I cited in the Introduction, compares joy and happiness and explains that "joy seems more closely related to aliveness than to happiness."

In Ginger Selander's doctoral thesis[2] *Joy in the world of caring* the author explains that joy gives meaning to life. She also talks about a deeper inner joy of life that is a fundamental frame of mind and attitude to life.

Results of a Survey on Joy of Life

As I was still not quite satisfied with what I had found about the meaning of the concepts of joy and joy of life I decided to ask some of my prospective readers what joy of life meant to them. I constructed a simple questionnaire and handed it out to my friends and their acquaintances.

34 people answered, 27 women and 7 men, of whom 24 were aged 60 years or older and 10 were under 60 years of age.

The questionnaire contained three open-ended questions. The first two questions read:

1. Describe what joy of life is to you and how it feels.
2. Give one or more examples of situations where you feel or have felt joy of life.

Many people found it difficult to answer the first question. Instead of describing *how* joy of life feels they described *when* they felt joy of life.

The most common term to describe the feeling of joy of life was *inner harmony*, which was mentioned by eight informants. Other common terms were *having a balance* and *being at peace*. Some informants talked about how they felt joy of life in their bodies.

- ❖ *Joy of life is when I feel happiness and peace flowing through my body.* (Woman, 60-69)
- ❖ *It's like something soft in my body.* (Woman, 80-89)

Is joy of life the same as being glad or joyous? A few people reflected on this and found that inner joy is stronger than being glad and that joy of life is *more lasting and deeper* than joy.

- ❖ *Maybe you could say that joy of life is more lasting than joy, or maybe something deeper that is not just there for the moment.* (Woman, 70-79)

Only a few informants mentioned any connection between joy of life and life. One man described *an intense feeling of living* that came after someone had died. Another man talked about when *it felt good to live* and when he enjoyed life. One woman mentioned the feeling that *life is worth living*, while another expressed *the joy of existing*. A third woman discussed *not giving up and dying before one's time*.

- *When it feels good to live and I enjoy life.* (Man, 30-39)
- *The joy of being alive.* (Woman, 60-69)

Others talked about being *active, healthy* and *independent*. Active meant doing things they enjoyed. Being healthy referred to both mental and physical health, while independent meant being financially secure and able to take care of themselves, to wake up in the morning ready to experience a new day and being able to live in their own home.

Many talked about how *connecting with nature* enabled them to feel the joy of life. They mentioned sitting by the sea or walking on the shore, taking long walks alone and walking in the woods. Struggling with nature could also lead to the joy of life, in the same way as the experience of breath-taking scenery, wonderful winter days and sunny summer mornings.

- *To sit by the sea, watching the water.* (Woman, 60-69)
- *To walk in the woods. To struggle with nature, for example climbing a mountain or kayaking when there is a strong wind.* (Man, 80-90)
- *Enjoying breath-taking scenery.* (Woman, 50-59)

A few people talked about *God*. A woman described her gratefulness to God and how she could feel it in her whole body. Other examples were praying or listening to music in a church.

Being *pleased with oneself and one's situation* was another way of describing joy of life. Several people considered it important to *feel safe* and some also mentioned *expectations of the future*.

> ❖ *Joy of life has to do with feeling safe in my daily life but also reconciliation with the past and confidence in the future.* (Man, 60-69)

In their responses to all three questions almost every informant mentioned the importance of a good relationship with their *family*, for example children, grandchildren and spouses, as a source of joy of life.

Here are some quotations about family members.

> ❖ *I experience joy when I see my family experience joy.* (Woman, 40-49)
> ❖ *When I do something special together with my grand-children.* (Woman, 60-69)
> ❖ *Every time I have some magical moments with my kids, even if it is just looking at how beautiful they are when they are asleep.* (Woman, 40-49)
> ❖ *Doing things together with my husband.* (Woman, 60-69)

Many informants also talked a great deal about *friends*. A friend is someone you care about and who cares about you. A good friend shows an interest in what is going on in your life, how you think and feel about things and accepts you for who you are. Here are a couple of quotations from my survey about situations when friends contribute to the feeling of joy of life.

> ❖ *Going to work and meeting my best friend and colleague after a few weeks on holiday.* (Woman, 60-69)
> ❖ *Sharing bad and good days with friends.* (Woman, 50-59)

The informants in the survey also expressed a wish to get to know *new and interesting people* for example by travelling and to avoid "energy thieves". The following are some quotations about that:

> ❖ *Having an intellectual exchange with someone, or travelling.* (Woman, 60-69)

❖ *When I am in a country I have never been to before and see a relationship between people, for example an adult and a child, and I realize that it works in about the same way as with me and my grandchild. When I am happy about a child's happiness.* (Woman, 70-79)

The third open-ended question was:

3. What would you like to do or what would have to happen to increase your joy of life?

Not surprisingly, many answers concerned the informants' *health*. They talked about staying healthy or recovering from present illnesses. Other issues were *being accepted for who they are, being pleased with themselves, accepting their body, obtaining more variation in life, becoming reconciled with the past* and *being aware of the particular aspects of living at the end of life*.

One woman, aged 60-69, stated that she was pleased with her life and did not want anything else.

In answer to the question concerning how they could improve their joy of life in the future, many people talked about *relationships* with other people, for example children, grandchildren and friends, while a few wanted to find a soul-mate.

Is joy of life important? The questionnaire also contained a couple of questions on the importance of joy of life. I wanted to know how important the informants found joy of life and how much joy of life they felt.

The results revealed that the informants' subjective experience of feeling joy of life was much less than their subjective experience of how important it is. To 29 people it was very important and to 3 people fairly important. On the question about how much joy of life they feel only 9 answered very much and 14 fairly much.

Conclusion

In summary, the 34 informants, most of them women aged over 60, stated that joy of life was very important to them. They found it difficult to describe the feeling of joy of life but easy to mention situations in which they experienced it. Joy of life is no doubt a complicated concept. Many of the informants described joy in certain situations rather than an inner deep and long lasting feeling of joy of life in their bodies.

Before ending this chapter and starting to describe the keys to more joy of life, I would like to summarize how I define the concept:

> Joy of life is a choice that gives us a perspective from which we can view life as a whole. It is an internal feeling. You can feel it in your body as something soft or as a sensation of harmony, balance and peace. Joy of life is something greater and deeper than happiness, it has no objective and it includes a desire to live.

KEY 1: SELF-KNOWLEDGE

I think of life as a good book. The further you get into it, the more it begins to make sense.
Harold Kushner

Who have I become and who would I like to be? These are two very important questions, whether you are about to retire, recently retired or if you are middle-aged and have many years left before retirement but for other reasons are trying to figure out what to do with the rest of your life. We should all ask ourselves these questions now and then. You can be sure of one thing: you are not the same person today as you were at the age of twenty or thirty. You have changed. But who are you now? Of course, parts of you are the same. You have talents that have not changed at all. Maybe some of your early dreams are still your dreams.

But you have changed a great deal because of all the experiences you have had over many years. With age people become more and more different from other people in their peer group. The older we are the more we differ as individuals compared to other people of the same age. This process of becoming different from other people of your age group starts long before retirement age. All adults are very different as individuals. I want you to bear that in mind while reading this book.

In addition, our life circumstances vary a great deal. Many of us do not enjoy perfect health and even if we do we may have a spouse who is disabled, elderly parents to take care of, young children or adult children who need help with their own children. Most of us, whether younger and older, do not have the financial resources to do whatever we like. Life is not perfect or fair. All this may limit your freedom and opportunities. My point here is that you still have a choice concerning how to live the rest of your life and it is up to you to decide if you want to live by chance or by choice.

Who Have I Become?

What I do today is important because I am paying a day of my life for it. What I accomplish must be worthwhile because the price is high.
Author unknown

Who have you become? I am not the first person to consider this an important question. Many authors of self-help books tell you to ask the same question but it is worth repeating. The question is always relevant, especially if you are experiencing a transition or change in your life situation for any reason. Examples are an empty nest when your children move out, going through a divorce or the death of someone close, loss of your job or a change in your career. You must ask yourself "Who have you become?" because if you do not know who you are, you can never make the best of the rest of your life and use all the opportunities available. You can choose to feel sorry for yourself or decide to face up to new challenges. There are many things out there to discover, to learn, to be a part of and you are free to choose within the limits of your circumstances.

Do you get annoyed, stressed and tired when you hear about all the opportunities that are available? Would you prefer to take it easy, enjoy one day at a time without the pressure you had earlier in your life? Fine. That is wonderful! It is completely OK not to have a calendar that is full and it is equally OK to prefer not to have a host of plans. It is your choice just as it is your choice to be busier than ever. Remember, we are all different! How much or what we do is not important. How we feel when we do what we do is crucial!

If you have more leisure time now because you have retired or your children have moved out you might prefer doing nothing much at all. As a senior, a reason might be that you are still enjoying "an extended holiday". This could last for six or twelve months and be wonderful. You enjoy it so much and say to yourself that your life has never been better. But my intention with this book is to help you with all the years following your first year as a retired senior or as a parent with an empty nest.

You may experience that there are people in your life who envy you for your free time and believe that they can dispose of it. In that case you must speak out and stop them. The same goes for people who tell you to do what they enjoy doing. You are in charge and can decide whether you want to take it easy or get more out of life. Once again, it is your choice.

If you do not know what you would like to do with the time and opportunities that are available there is a risk that you will just be killing time. Time passes anyway and it is limited and irreplaceable, so you had better choose wisely. We all know that our days are numbered, so why would we ever want to kill time?

Killing time means that you feel bored, which is the opposite of joy of life. Of course we are all bored sometimes, including myself. Boredom can be good for you. It may mean that you have stopped putting yourself under stress trying to do too many things at the same time. Maybe boredom helps you activate yourself with something that will bring you joy. Even boredom is a choice. Awareness of this choice is a first step to being bored less often and experiencing more joy of life. But perhaps you have no idea why you are bored. What or who is so boring? Is it life itself? Could it be because of you?

The opposite of boredom is living a passionate life. To do that you first of all have to find out what your passions are.

Maybe you are now thinking: "Yes, I would like to get to know the person I have become but how can I do that?" Wanting to know is a good start and if you realize that it might be useful for you it is even better. Here are a few things you can do:

- o Listen to your self-talk and your thoughts.

- Talk to someone you know, such as a trusted friend.
- Reflect.
- Pay attention to your gut feeling.
- Accept who you are!

You can also ask yourself questions such as:

- What is most important to me in my life?
- Which persons are most important to me in my life?
- What makes me happy?
- What makes me sad?
- What makes me feel good?
- What makes me bored?

Here are some more questions:

- Do I complain too much?
- Am I as grateful as I should be for what I have in my life?
- Do I say "I am sorry" and "forgive me"?
- Am I continually learning something new?

Maybe earlier in your life you thought that when you have a great deal of time you will do this or that, things you did not have time to do before. But what happens? You have the time and still do not do all those things that you thought you longed to do. That can be an example of the fact that you have changed or that you did not know yourself. You need such discoveries to understand who you are and have become in order to make your future choices.

There may also be other reasons when you don't take action. Here are some common excuses to reflect on:

- *It's too complicated or difficult.* But you have already successfully completed so many difficult tasks in your life. Why not now?
- *I am tired.* Doing nothing is tiring too. Maybe you need some rest, maybe you don't sleep enough.

- *It's boring.* Is it? How do you know if you haven't ever tried?
- *I do not know where to start.* Start where you are right now. Go forward step by step.
- *What would other people think?* What other people think is their problem and not yours. Let them think whatever they want.

Another piece of advice is to distinguish between what you do and who you are. The question "Who am I?" is about identity. Our talents are part of our identity. So here are some more questions:

- What am I good at?
- What am I less good at?
- What did I do yesterday or this week that was me at my best?

The easiest answers to the question Who have I become? concern the different roles we play. It may be about what job you have, your family situation, sports or other leisure activities that you participate in. You are a teacher, married, the mother of two children etc. All those roles are very important but they only partly answer the question about who you have become.

Your self-confidence and self-esteem, your passions, your attitudes and values, your limiting beliefs and fears are all part of who you have become and I will come back to that in this and the following chapters.

The act of writing things down has a great deal of power - some experts say 5 times, some say 50 times and some even say 1,000 times more power than thoughts alone! Writing helps you organize your thoughts. Therefore I am going to ask you many times in this book to write things down. Below are a few examples. Remember to do this for just a short period or now and then. Otherwise there is a risk that you will stop after a while because you get tired of doing it:

- Start every day by writing down 3-5 good things that you will achieve in the course of the day.

- o In the evening, write down what you did especially well that day.
- o Record your strengths and weaknesses.

Self-esteem and Self-confidence

No one can make you feel inferior without your consent.
Eleanor Roosevelt

Self-esteem refers to how you feel about yourself in general and develops from experiences and situations that shaped how you look at yourself today. Low self-esteem usually starts very early in people's lives, often before the age of six years. When children hear or see something from people around them that makes them think they are not good enough or lovable, they may start believing that something is wrong with them.

Sometimes this view of yourself is based on a mere misunderstanding. Once a child gains the impression that she/he is not good enough she/he starts searching for proof that it is true and finally accepts that such images are correct and believes that it cannot be changed. The child has thus developed limiting beliefs. I will talk more about these in the next chapter.

Nathaniel Branden[1] states that self-esteem is confidence in our ability to think, in our ability to cope with the challenges of life and in our right to succeed and be happy and that we deserve it! Branden writes that the essence of self-esteem is to trust our minds and to be aware that we are worthy of happiness, which inspires motivation to act.

When we have high self-esteem we can better cope with the challenges and hardships in our lives. High self-esteem makes you more willing to accept challenges to get more out of life.

Branden also states that self-esteem, whether high or low, tends to result in self-fulfilling prophecies. When you trust and respect yourself you send out signals that increase your chances of people responding in a respectful way, thus increasing your self-esteem. If you lack self-respect and are treated in a less respectful way your self-esteem becomes even lower.

Low self-esteem can result in depression, frustration and anger, fear, too much worrying and negativity. Another consequence may be that you do not stand up for yourself for fear of causing trouble and that the goals you set are far too low or no goals at all. Furthermore, it may mean that you feel unfulfilled and indecisive, perhaps even unloved and unlovable.

Having low self-esteem may be so subtle that you are not aware of it until something very bad happens. So how do you know that you have low self-esteem? There are some warning signs. For example, if you cannot handle praise well or if you cannot say no to people when they ask you to do something. Other signs are blaming others or apologizing when there is no reason to do so.

We talk to ourselves every day and if our self-talk is negative our self-esteem diminishes. But you can change what you say to yourself. Start by listening to your self-talk.

When your self-esteem increases you start to set yourself higher goals, you have higher expectations and put in more effort, therefore you will achieve more and further increase your self-esteem. Focus on what you have done well.

Self-confidence is how you feel about your abilities and can vary from situation to situation. By focusing on the things you are confident in you can improve both your self-esteem and self-confidence.

To increase your confidence and self-esteem you need to have something to look forward to and know that you have what it takes to get there.

Think about the good qualities other people say you have. Could they be right and you wrong? If you start believing that you are going in the right direction. Trust your intuition. Associate with positive people and act enthusiastically. You will then train your brain to be more enthusiastic.

You must also realize that you are not the only one who makes mistakes and has flaws. Everybody has flaws and everybody makes mistakes because we are human and therefore not perfect. Learn from it instead of getting stuck in self-pity. Focus on the aspects of a situation that you feel good about and managed well. Did you do your best? Then you have a reason to be proud of yourself. If you acknowledge what you did well, you can use your mistakes to your own benefit and turn them into advantages by learning from them. Deal with the mistake, learn from it and move on! If you never failed it means that you never tried.

Failure offers you all the experiences, feelings and thoughts you can obtain from whatever endeavour you set out to undertake. These will be with you for your whole life so embrace them. Your failures are there for you. Look upon them as your allies that are going to prepare you for success at the perfect time. Failure shows that you are going in the right direction and prepares you for something bigger. Failure reminds you that you had the courage to try. The real failure is not giving yourself a chance to try. Don't be afraid to try. Embrace your mistakes. Once you have become comfortable with the possibility of failure it will be easier for you to take risks.

A setback that you learn from will make you stronger and bring you closer to achieving your goals. You learn what did not work. Compare yourself with children who are learning to walk. They fall all the time, get up again and with every false step they get closer to being able to walk. Repetition is the mother of learning and children learn very much by repetition. So can you! Being comfortable with the possibility of failure means that you may find it easier to take calculated risks.

Building good relationships may help you to become more confident. Being grateful for who you are may also have positive effects. Furthermore, it is important to feel that you are worthy. Otherwise you will probably not obtain the outcome you are seeking in different areas of your life. If you do not feel that you are worthy enough to have the best, you will find many ways to sabotage your efforts and fail to obtain the best.

To increase your self-confidence you also have to give yourself permission to be exactly as you are right now. Find peace with who you are. Make a list of 10-20 things that you have achieved in your life. Be proud of all you have accomplished so far.

You can also list your qualities and strengths to help create more self-confidence. Remember that your potential is almost unlimited and that you can more or less be the person you want to be.

Ask yourself:

- What did I learn from the mistake?
- How can I avoid making the same mistake again?
- What did I do well?

If you value yourself, you understand that you are a gift to anyone you meet.
Rhonda Britten

Who Would I Like to Be?

If you do not know where you want to go, you will end up anywhere life takes you.
Joe Rubino

When I was about to retire I found the question about who I would like to be very exciting. Of course the question was not new as I had often asked myself questions about my professional dreams and career opportunities. That may be the most important question for you right now. But what made it new for me as a senior was that I had not thought very much about me, or other seniors, as people who change and grow as a person. This must have been an example of a stereotype conception and prejudice that I was simply not aware of. We all have them. What prejudices do you have?

Who you would like to be has very much to do with who you are now and your knowledge of who you have become. It is also associated with your life circumstances. You must start where you are now. This is especially true when life takes a turn, when you lose your job or someone close to you. It is time for dreams to come to the surface and for you to take care of yourself. If you are about to retire, it is time to leave job titles behind and find a new identity. Discovering who you have become and who you would like to be is a process that takes time but it is worth it, if you want to live a life of choice and not of chance.

Who you would like to be concerns how you want to spend your days, what kind of a person you want to see when you look at yourself in the mirror and also who you would like to be remembered as.

You may have to deal with the necessity of increasing your self-esteem and self-confidence. You might have to find out what limiting beliefs you have that need to be changed because they are sabotaging the realization of who you would like to be.

Here are a few questions to ask yourself:

- Where and with what do I want to spend my time and energy?
- What are my life priorities?
- What made me proud of myself in the past?
- What can I do to make me proud of myself in the future?
- How can I contribute to making this world a better place?
- What would I like to learn?
- For what would I like to be remembered?

Here are some more questions:

- What kind of a person am I?
- Am I a positive or negative person?
- What do other people say that they like about me? Ask someone who knows you well!
- Have my values changed or would I like them to change in the future?
- Do I want to be a person who has a meaningful life?

- o To whom or what would I like to contribute and with what?
- o What is my purpose here on earth and how can I enrich the lives of others?

Wholeheartedly listening to the answers to these questions, as well as to your experiences and memories may eliminate some of your doubts. You will stop being uncertain. When you have a deep understanding of who you are and would like to be, you will know what to do.

Write a speech for your 100th birthday from someone who knows you well. This is what we recommend people who take The Passion Test[2] to do. It is a way of clarifying what you want from the rest of your life, who you are and what legacy you want to leave behind.

Some people who take The Passion Test do not want to write such a speech or do not want to think of themselves as being 100 years old. If you also feel like that you can choose another future birthday, for example 60, 70 or 80.

Another powerful exercise is to write a letter to a friend or relative. Date the letter five, ten or more years from now and tell your friend or relative about your life at the imagined future date.

You can also use visualization in the way many sportspeople do to win a game or a race. Visualization is a tool that can be useful for improving many areas. You imagine a future situation that you want to manage well, for example making a presentation or being successful in a job interview. You create a mental picture of yourself in the situation, feeling relaxed, enjoying the task and doing it well. You should then repeat this mental picture or rehearsal many times.

Passions

There is no passion to be found playing small – in settling for a life that is less than the one you are capable of living.
Nelson Mandela

Not all of us know what we really want, despite the fact that knowing what we want is a key to obtaining it. Many of us who are still working are not certain about what we want in terms of employment and career and maybe we are even more unsure about what we want when our children have left the nest or we retire or have more free time for other reasons. No wonder! You are used to being very busy and now for various reasons you are no longer as busy and can choose what to do with your spare time. Maybe you do not wish to admit that you don't know what you want. Instead you tell friends and yourself that you are so busy and have so much to do! That's fine but how passionate are you about it and how meaningful is it? Do you have a sense of purpose in your life?

Once you know what your main passions are you can start living them. You use them as a filter in your life, meaning that whenever you're faced with a choice, a decision or an opportunity, you choose in favour of your passions.[3] In this way you can begin living passionately and have a strategy that you can use for the rest of your life for aligning with your passions and the things you are burning for. You will then live by choice and not by chance, thus experiencing more fulfilment and joy in your life.

In my experience of helping people to take The Passion Test[4], some find it difficult to list the ten or more passions that is the start of the process. A few even say that they have no passions at all. Some expect that they should know what they want. If you do not know your passions, it may be a sign of your lack of self-knowledge. Who have you become? Who would you like to be? Another reason for not knowing your passions may be the fact that we are trained to want more on the outside, while passions are about the inside.

So, what is passion? Passion is joy. Passion is what you are burning for. Passion is being excited and fascinated about things.

Passion is the fuel that drives you forward, what is important to you in life. Passion enables you to overcome obstacles and make your dreams reality. Passions make you come alive. Once you find your passions nothing will be able to stop you. It is that special feeling that throbs inside you and when you feel it, nothing else matters. Passion can be like a relationship with a very special person, who makes you feel relaxed and happy irrespective of the surrounding circumstances.

You can look at celebrities and learn from their happiness, success and confidence, not because they are rich or famous, but because they have passion. Passion is the key to being yourself, because passion changes you and allows you to automatically stand out from everyone else. Passion ignites what is in you, making you feel good about yourself and also unleashes your potential.

When you are trying to find your passions you focus on WHAT. What are you burning for? What makes you enthusiastic, what makes the time pass so quickly when you are doing what you are passionate about? Think big! Perhaps the dreams you had when you were young did not come true. Maybe there are things that you wished for and thought about throughout your life but never had the opportunity to realize.

Interestingly, once you are clear about WHAT and focus on it, HOW will emerge. I have experienced this myself several times and it has been amazing on each occasion. Examples are when I needed help with my new company and had no idea how to find it, help suddenly appeared as if by a miracle. When it became clear to me that I wanted to improve my relationship with some people who were important to me, I initially did not know how to go about it but very soon ways turned up. When it was clear to me that I wanted to learn more about writing a book, help came from the most unexpected direction.

When you find your passions you become enthusiastic, happy and joyous. However, you may find that people who are close to you such as your family members, your spouse and your friends are less excited than you are. In fact, they may turn out to be anything but supportive and instead become critical and judgmental. They may tell you that you are not being realistic, that they thought you were cleverer than that, what will people think of you and so on.

Barrie Davenport[5] reflected on why this happens and found that there may be many reasons. For example, they might feel threatened by your ability and courage. They might fear that if you fail it could impact on them in some way. They might feel jealous because you have found your passions and they have not. They might worry that you won't succeed or they simply do not understand your passions and how you can make them work.

Sometimes the people closest to you react out of concern for your or their own well-being. Nevertheless, there is a risk that you could lose friends or offend family members and experience unexpected reactions. On the other hand, your passions are likely to open the doors to new relationships with like-minded people who support your decisions. Passion may also give you a sense of belonging and the feeling of fitting in when you are together with people who share the same passion.

When I started my new company Senior Life Joy many people supported me. But I also experienced a few people who doubted me. The most discouraging contact I had was with the tax authorities, who informed me that they did not believe in me or my company and that I would never make any money. I spent a great deal of time writing long letters to them in order to explain my plans and try to convince them that my ideas and the future prospects of my company were good. That is an example of negative energy trying to deter me and had I not been as determined as I was, it could have made me give up.

The tax authorities adhered to rigid rules, used very bureaucratic language and did not seem to realize that if they supported me and wished me good luck, the chances of getting what they wanted, i.e., more tax from me, could increase. This is an example of the unexpected lack of understanding that you must be prepared to face once you have found your passions. However, you can learn from the experience and it may make you aware of the importance of supporting other people's passions, even when you do not fully believe in or understand them.

To find your passions ask yourself:

- o What are my strengths?
- o What are my unique talents?
- o What can I do better than others?
- o What makes my heart sing?
- o What can I do for hours without thinking about the time?
- o What fills me with energy?
- o What am I looking forward to?
- o What do I get excited about doing?

Meaning and Purpose

The meaning of life is a life of purpose.
Robert Byrne

Do you want a more meaningful life? If so, you are not alone. That is what most of us find important. We all want to make a difference at some level and leave a legacy behind. One of the informants in my survey on joy of life said:

❖ *To increase the joy of life I need to have a purpose and meaning in life.* (Woman, 60-69)

Unfortunately, even experts cannot provide a simple answer to the question of where we can find meaning. Each of us must find and bring meaning to our lives. However, it has been suggested that for most people there is a meaning in relationships, such as parents, children, grandchildren, partners and friends. My joy of life survey also revealed that doing things for other people can be meaningful and bring joy and happiness into your life.

Others have said that the meaning of life is to live a meaningful life.

To gain the sense of meaningfulness you must listen to yourself and refrain from doing things you do not want to do, despite what others tell you.

A meaningful life is not boring and increases your sense of value and being useful. Meaningful activities give you a feeling of developing and make you forget time and space. A lack of meaningfulness may result in boredom, tiredness and bitterness.

On the other hand, a meaningful life can be frightening as it may include risky and challenging activities. You might also need the courage to take risks.

Some researchers[6] concluded that older people who held the view that meaning matters were happier, kinder, more energetic, goal oriented and resilient, as well as tending to live longer.

Another study[7] showed that subjective wellbeing, i.e., life satisfaction, happiness, as well as a sense of purpose and meaning might have a role in both health maintenance and survival at an older age.

Ask yourself the following questions:

- Does meaning matter to me?
- What makes my life meaningful?
- Why am I here?

Passions, meaning and purpose are interconnected. When you find your passions you gain a sense of purpose in your life, which in turn makes your life meaningful. It is not what you do that is meaningful, but how passionately you do it and from which perspective you look at it. It is important whether you see the glass of water as half full or half empty. Seeing the glass as half full means that you can fill it up.

Having a purpose will help you in many ways. It enables you to remain physically healthy because you make efforts to maintain a healthy life style when you have a reason. Learning new things and using your brain to find solutions keeps you mentally fit. It helps you to work with things you believe in, leading to appreciation from others and confirmation that you are competent.

I expect that many of you have already heard the story of the three stonecutters, but I find it worth repeating.

Parable of the three stonecutters
Three young and strong stonecutters were asked what they were doing. the first replied, "i am making a living." the second kept on hammering while he said, "i am doing the best job of stonecutting in the entire country." the third one looked up with a visionary gleam in his eyes and said, "i am building a cathedral."[8]

When you have a purpose in your life, when your life and what you do feel meaningful to you, then your zest for life and wish to live increase and you will experience more joy of life. But to find purpose and meaningfulness you have to be open to change. That is the second key and you can learn about it in the following chapter.

You can live each day in a world filled with 'problems', or rise each morning and embrace a world filled with unseen solutions...eager for you to find them. The decision is yours...both worlds exist. The one you choose is the one you will create.
Michael McMillan

KEY 2: OPENNESS TO CHANGE

Feel the fear and do it anyway.
Susan Jeffers

Why Change?

Do we really have to change? Are we not good enough? What is change all about? Firstly, it is important to stress that yes, we are good enough! We are all amazing and unique individuals. There has never been anyone like you and there will never be anyone like you.

Secondly, it is important to be aware of the fact that we do not change our personality or life experiences. When we speak about change we are often referring to behavioural changes. Sometimes we change our values, our thoughts and our perspectives. We may alter our attitude to ourselves, our need for change and to be more positive. We may change our priorities when we realize that we want to live our lives more aligned with our passions and with more joy of life. Change is also very much about learning and reformulating the questions in life.

How you react to change depends on whether you are actively searching for or actively avoiding it. The first step is to be aware of a need or wish to change. The next step is to decide what to change to, which can be difficult. It can also happen that you have conflicting ideas about where or what you want to be after the change. You should create a picture of the outcome.

Bringing about change may be difficult or painful, so you must feel and realize that it is for your own benefit. Occasionally you change without being aware of the reasons. For example, I quit smoking only weeks before I received my lung cancer diagnosis. Why? I am not sure. Two people I knew died of lung cancer not long before, which might have been a trigger on a subconscious level. I never admitted that I was afraid of getting lung cancer myself. I just quit smoking!

At other times you are very aware of the need for change. There are things that do not work well in your life. Other people may have said something that had an impact on you, such as your children, grandchildren or other people's children. Children are good at being honest with you!

Another way to learn about the need for change is by having role models. You see and realize what other people can do and have, so you want to be like them. Maybe you are a role model yourself or would like to be and therefore you need to change in order to live up to that ideal.

Changing may mean taking risks, which requires courage. Stepping outside your comfort zone is obviously frightening, challenging and uncomfortable, but it is the only way to learn, grow and move forward towards unimaginable rewards.

If you change, what will your life be like in one, five or ten years? If you do not change, what will the future be? Thinking of the long term consequences will make it easier to step outside your comfort zone. The danger of not doing so is that you fail to grow as a person. Every opportunity and experience in life, whether good or bad, enables you to learn something, either about yourself or about those around you.

But what if you choose to stay in your comfort zone and have no wish to change? Allow yourself to be pleased with that alternative, too! The important thing is that you make a conscious choice. One of my older informants in the survey said:

- ❖ *At my age you feel joy of life when there aren't too many changes.* (Woman, 70-79)

If you feel reluctant to change it might be a good idea to investigate the reasons. Are you reluctant to change per se or just in certain areas? Could it have to do with low self-esteem? Are you reluctant to face an unknown and uncertain outcome or the change process itself? Asking yourself questions about your reluctance can be a way of discovering who you are now.

Seniors may find change even more difficult than younger people, as they tend to be more stuck in their patterns. That is what people in general and especially older people often think.

In reality, older people have to adjust to many difficult changes, such as retirement, illness, as well as the death of family members and friends. They simply have to manage to live with change and they do!

There is a wonderful saying that states:

The person who says it cannot be done should not interrupt the person doing it.
Chinese proverb

I remember that when I was 55 years old and had recently completed my PhD I had to carry out what in my view were really boring tasks because of staffing cuts at my work place. I disliked my job intensely and was not positive at all. In fact, I was extremely negative and was probably regarded as reluctant to change by my colleagues and managers. At the same time I was planning to move for a year to a university in England. This implied a change of country, language, career, accommodation, indeed practically everything! Was I a person who was reluctant to change? I learnt from that experience that we should be very careful when we label people as inflexible and resistant to change!

If you think that you are too old to change or to realize your dreams because you will be 50, 60 or 70 years old next year, then remember that you will be 50, 60 or 70 next year irrespective of whether or not you change. You grow old when you lose interest in life and cease to dream, not because of your chronological age.

Some people have the most productive and happiest years of their lives after the age of 65 or even when they are over 80. Could that be you? Don't forget the saying that what people regret when they look back on their lives is in most cases what they failed to do, rather than what they did.

Role models are important for all of us, irrespective of our age. Write a list of people you know who have been active and successful within different areas, for example:

- Relatives
- Friends and neighbours
- Artists, writers, athletes
- Scientists
- Famous people, for example Nelson Mandela, Mother Teresa, Mahatma Gandhi.

Your expectations are important as we tend to get what we expect. If you expect to be successful your chances of doing well will increase, while if you expect not to do very well your chances of failure increase too. What you think can change your life. You will become what you think about.

Thinking that it is too late to change or to realize your dreams happens to all of us. It is a very handy excuse for not trying. On most occasions it is not too late but of course it can be.

I read in the newspaper about a man who celebrated his 70th birthday. He said that he had always thought he would die young, but now it was too late!

Change can signify growing as a person and growth is really amazing because sometimes there are no signs of growth at all and yet you are growing. That is what the following story is about.

The Moso Bamboo Tree
The moso is a bamboo plant that grows in China and the far east. After the moso is planted, no visible growth occurs for up to five years – even under ideal conditions!

Then, as if by magic, it suddenly begins growing at the rate of nearly two and a half feet per day, reaching a full height of ninety feet within six weeks.

But it's not magic. The moso's rapid growth is due to the miles of roots it develops during those first five years, five years of getting ready.

How deep do your roots go? Are you ready?
Joel Weldon[1]

Limiting Beliefs

You have to help yourself first! Limiting beliefs lead to limiting lives!
Rich and Susann Crawford

If you observe your thoughts, you will find that many of them are judgments on other people or yourself, which may be limiting and sabotage your life. These thoughts are called limiting beliefs. We all have such beliefs about what we can and cannot do. Limiting beliefs are very powerful and stop us from being who we are and can be. They are lies that act as chains and hold us back.

When you were young, many people such as parents, siblings, teachers, peers and other influential individuals may have told you that your dreams were childish, that you did not deserve them or that you would never see them come true. They may have added that you were not intelligent, beautiful, strong, worthy or whatever.

You started to believe it. As I mentioned earlier, that is how you developed low self-esteem and how limiting beliefs entered your life and started to restrict and sabotage it. Since then such beliefs have controlled your life and held you back. Our beliefs result in pain, failure, being in a rut and unhappy and we are unaware of most of them.

Another way of expressing it is to say that we get in our own way and sabotage ourselves because of limiting beliefs and habits that are not good for us, something we all do at times.

It is no use blaming those people from your childhood who said these things, because they had their own limiting beliefs and their intention may have been good. Instead, you must realize that while your childhood might not have been perfect, it is over. Instead, you should attempt to identify your limiting beliefs and start changing them. It is not easy to change our thoughts but being aware of the benefit of doing so is a first step. Starting with very small changes is another way.

Much of what you say to yourself, your inner conversation, is on a sub-conscious level, so in order to start changing your limiting beliefs you have to choose situations that you know you are negative about. For example, maybe you tell yourself that you cannot learn a foreign language because you were told that your mother was not good at learning languages. Thus, you believe that you inherited this problem and there is no point even trying. However, you can change these thoughts to "I am going to try anyway."

You can also write down some of your beliefs and start questioning them. For example, if you believe that rich people are selfish try to think of rich people you know or have heard of who are very generous. Could that be true? Could the truth be that some rich people are selfish and others are not? Could your belief about rich people being selfish be a reason why you don't have much money? Perhaps you just don't want to be a selfish person.

Here are a few more examples of common self-limiting beliefs:

- o I am not clever enough
- o It would be selfish to want more
- o I don't deserve it
- o I am too old

Later in this book I will present more examples of limiting beliefs.

Sometimes the hardest part of the journey is believing you are worthy of the trip.
Glenn Beck

Instead of trying to listen to and question our thoughts there is a risk of us blaming other people or thinking that we are unlucky. Perhaps you believe that some people are born lucky and others not. Do you think that you belong to those who have no luck or that you have had some luck but fear that it will run out at any minute?

Could it be that unlucky people are unlucky because they believe they are? That they focus on what they don't have and aren't getting instead of focusing on what they want and how to get it?

Being lucky is about believing that you make your own luck. You get what you think. Change your luck by changing your thoughts. When you have positive thoughts, focus on things you desire, take action with joy and believe that you have what it takes to achieve what you desire, then you will be lucky.

Do you believe that lucky people have more joy in their lives than unlucky people? I believe so. But I also believe that people who have joy in their lives have more luck.

Here is a story about luck.

Good Luck and Bad Luck.
There was once a wise farmer who knew that life's experiences are often not what they appear. He owned a beautiful mare that was the finest in the entire village. One day, someone left the corral gate open and the mare ran off. The villagers said to the farmer, "What terrible luck." The wise farmer replied, "Good luck, bad luck, who can tell." Several days later, the mare returned with a beautiful herd of wild stallions accompanying her. The villagers marveled at what good luck the farmer had. Again, the wise old man observed, "Good luck, bad luck, who can tell."

One day, the farmer's only son was out in the yard breaking in the wild stallions. When he was thrown from his horse and broke his shoulder, the villagers remarked, "What terrible luck." Once again, as he was wont to do, the farmer said, "Good luck, bad luck, who can tell." A week later, the government declared war, calling into service all able-bodied men from the village. All went to war with the exception of the farmer's son, who was still healing from his injury. When all the young soldiers from the village were caught in an ambush and killed, the villagers again remarked to the farmer, "What good luck that your son broke his shoulder and was spared." And the story goes on.

Good and bad, right and wrong are merely interpretations that we attach to experiences. As with all opposites, we cannot have one without the other. All of life's experiences present themselves as tools for our own creation. It is entirely up to us to decide how we will experience any aspect of life as it presents us with an opportunity to decide who we choose to be. Instead of being a victim of what life presents us, we can choose to be the source, the creator of how we will respond and how we will be affected by the challenge. Our response is our opportunity to define who we choose to be.[2]

To be lucky, you have to keep your eyes open so that you can identify and seize opportunities when they turn up. It also concerns creating new opportunities. The more opportunities you recognize and create the luckier you will be! You may also have to use your intuition to be able to identify opportunities.

Here is story about how difficult it can be to recognize an opportunity.

The Touchstone
When the great library of Alexandria burned, as the story goes, one book was saved. But it was not a valuable book; and so a poor man, who could read a little, bought it for a few coppers.

The book wasn't very interesting, but between its pages there was something very interesting indeed. It was a thin strip of vellum on which was written the secret of the "Touchstone"!

The touchstone was a small pebble that could turn any common metal into pure gold. The writing explained that it was lying among thousands and thousands of other pebbles that looked exactly like it. But the secret was this: The real stone would feel warm, while ordinary pebbles are cold.

So the man sold his few belongings, bought some simple supplies, camped on the seashore, and began testing pebbles.

He knew that if he picked up ordinary pebbles and threw them down again because they were cold, he might pick up the same pebble hundreds of times. So, when he felt one that was cold, he threw it into the sea. He spent a whole day doing this but none of them was the touchstone. Yet he went on and on this way. Pick up a pebble. Cold - throw it into the sea. Pick up another. Throw it into the sea.

The days stretched into weeks and the weeks into months. One day, however, about mid-afternoon, he picked up a pebble and it was warm. He threw it into the sea before he realized what he had done. He had formed such a strong habit of throwing each pebble into the sea that when the one he wanted came along, he still threw it away.

Author unknown[3]

What we can learn from this story is that unless we are observant, it is easy to fail to recognize an opportunity and just as easy to throw it away.

Ask yourself the following questions:

- Do I feel inferior to my friends and relatives?
- Do I believe that I was born unlucky?
- Do I feel that I do not measure up?
- Do I feel that I do not deserve to be happy and successful?
- How can I improve my ability to identify an opportunity?

Before I conclude this section about limiting beliefs I would like to remind you of all the good and positives statements about yourself that you probably heard as a child. Most of us did not only have people around us who taught us that we were stupid or not worthy.

Think about it! Who showed you that she/he believed in you or said encouraging words to you? Nobody? Are you sure?

Once you accept limiting beliefs it becomes difficult to believe in enabling beliefs but fortunately most of us do not only have negative beliefs that influence our lives but also positive beliefs if we are willing to see them and let them help us in our adult life.

Somebody, it might have been a teacher, a sports coach or a grandmother, did believe in you and tried to encourage you. Reflect on it! What positive and encouraging words do you recall and from whom?

When I look back on my life, my most important and positive beliefs probably came from my father. I have the impression that he believed in me so much that for him there were no limits. I had the capacity to achieve anything I wanted. Yes, I know that is fortunate! But it did not mean that I had excessive self-confidence, especially when I was young. However, when I look back now, I appreciate his belief in me so very much.

I would like you to reflect on your own enabling beliefs and not only on your limiting beliefs.

o What enabling beliefs did you acquire during your childhood? From whom?
o How can you enhance your enabling beliefs so that they have a greater influence on your life?

Attitudes

Attitude is a little thing that makes a big difference.
Winston Churchill

How you look upon yourself may have to do with your attitude. Are you a negative or a positive person? What do the people around you think about you? There is no doubt that a positive attitude is good for your health and positive feelings give you energy. Good health makes you feel better, which results in more joy, thus people will enjoy being around you, making you feel happy and further improving your health. It is an upward spiral. Having a positive attitude to yourself may be more important for your health than being physically fit and might influence your life expectancy. Even in crises, optimistic people remain mentally healthier. Besides, life is easier to live when you have a positive attitude.

A recent study by Bethany Kok and Barbara Fredrickson, referred to by Lauren Klein[4] in her article "How Positive Emotions Improve Our Health", showed that positive emotions improve our health by making people feel more socially connected. Thus, the key factor is the effect of positive emotions on our sense of connection to others. If we cannot connect with other people, we might achieve a similar effect by cultivating positive emotions on our own. As we experience more positive emotions over time, we may be taking care of both body and mind.

Ask yourself:

- Do I have a self-defeating mindset?
- Do I believe everything my mind is telling me?
- Is my mind telling me negative things?

Your attitude towards yourself is associated with your limiting beliefs. When you believe that other people think positively about you, you will act differently to how you would behave if you believe they have a negative opinion of you. Here is another quotation from Winston Churchill:

An optimist sees an opportunity in every calamity; a pessimist sees a calamity in every opportunity.
Winston Churchill

Seeing an opportunity in the difficulties you are faced with and having a positive and optimistic outlook on life will enable you to be happier and stop complaining. Complaining makes you sad and wastes your time. Focus on problem-solving instead. Remember, nobody can make you unhappy or miserable unless you allow them to do so. We should not underestimate the power of positive thinking. It is not what happens to you that is important, it is how you choose to look at it and respond.

Here is a story about an old lady and her positive attitude.

I Love It!
The 92-year-old, petite, well-poised and proud lady, who is fully dressed each morning by eight o'clock with her hair fashionably coiffed and makeup perfectly applied even though she is legally blind, moved to a nursing home today. Her husband of 70 years recently passed away, making the move necessary.

After many hours of waiting patiently in the lobby of the nursing home, she smiled sweetly when told her room was ready. As she maneuvered her walker to the elevator, I provided a visual description of her tiny room, including the eyelet sheets that had been hung on her window. "I love it," she stated with the enthusiasm of an eight-year-old having just been presented with a new puppy.

"Mrs. Jones, you haven't seen the room...just wait." "That doesn't have anything to do with it," she replied. "Happiness is something you decide on ahead of time. Whether I like my room or not doesn't depend on how the furniture is arranged. It's how I arrange my mind. I already decided to love it. It's a decision I make every morning when I wake up. I have a choice: I can spend the day in bed recounting the difficulty I have with the parts of my body that no longer work, or I can get out of bed and be thankful for the ones that do. Each day is a gift, and as long as my eyes open I'll focus on the new day and all the happy memories I've stored away...just for this time in my life."[5]

Optimism is a generally positive approach to life. Thinking positively and being optimistic means that you focus on what you want and how to get it, not on what you don't want and who to blame. You are not a problem solver but a solution finder, i.e., you focus on solutions. You ask yourself how you can deal with challenges instead of just worrying about them. You also look for the good in situations and people. Optimism is learned. However, thinking positively can be challenging. You may have doubts and believe that you are neither optimistic nor pessimistic but just realistic.

Maybe you think that it is better to have a pessimistic or realistic view on life than an optimistic one, as it means you will not be disappointed. That is a good point. However, being positive and optimistic does not mean that you should be naïve or anticipate that your expectations will always come true. Things go wrong. That's life and sometimes it is very useful to have a plan B. An optimistic mindset means that you have faith in your ability to realize your ambitions. This faith influences your thoughts, feelings and actions. Believing that you can means that you make greater efforts, thus increasing your chances of success and joy of life.

Being optimistic does not mean ignoring problems but thinking about them in a different way to a pessimist. Unlike a pessimist, you don't consider problems permanent and inevitable. Instead you see them as temporary and don't believe that positive experiences are due to luck or coincidence. As an optimist you are aware of your role in what is happening.

A way of starting to think more positively is to identify and write a list of things that you want to happen. Furthermore, it is important how we explain what is happening to us. Do we blame circumstances? Do we blame ourselves when negative events occur?

Many of us are used to putting others first and do not care enough for ourselves. We have learnt that it is selfish to put ourselves before others. Thus, we do not care for ourselves as much as we should. But caring for ourselves is actually necessary because it enables us to function better and we can be of more assistance to others when we feel good about ourselves.

Is most of your time devoted to others or yourself? The habit of putting others before ourselves can serve as an excuse and a way of blaming others, which prevents us from growing as a person. For the same reason you shouldn't blame yourself for things that are not your fault. We all fail and can learn from it. It does not mean that you are not good enough and it is not a reason to give up. Instead, you should just move on and try again or do something else.

Enjoy the following story about attitude being everything.

Your Attitude is Everything
There once was a woman who woke up one morning, looked in the mirror, and noticed she had only three hairs on her head. "Well", she said, "I think I'll braid my hair today." So she did and she had a wonderful day.

The next day she woke up, looked in the mirror and saw that she had only two hairs on her head. "H-M-M," she said, "I think I'll part my hair down the middle today." So she did and she had a grand day.

The next day she woke up, looked in the mirror and noticed that she had only one hair on her head. "Well" she said, "today I'm going to wear my hair in a pony tail." So she did and she had a fun, fun day.

The next day she woke up, looked in the mirror and noticed that there wasn't a single hair on her head. "YEA!" she exclaimed, "I don't have to fix my hair today!"
Author unknown [6]

Thinking more positively about things is a way of finding greater joy of life, which was also stated by one of the informants in my survey, a woman aged 30-39. The biggest obstacle in your life is in your head. You become a more positive person when you speak positively and express uplifting thoughts, as well as when you praise and compliment others. The more positive thoughts you have, the less room there is for negative thoughts.

Some of our negative thoughts are subconscious so you don't know how negative you are. Start with those negative thoughts you are aware of and try to change them into more positive thoughts. You can reformulate your thoughts. For example, if you think "I am not good enough" you can change it into "I am good enough." Then you need to repeat "I am good enough" several times every day for some time until you have finally changed your limiting belief into a positive one.

You can once again make use of the power of writing. Make a note in the morning about the thoughts that entered your mind when you awoke. Are they negative or positive? Positive thoughts are better as how you view your life and yourself in the morning has a major impact on the rest of your day.

Another strategy for becoming more positive is to think about your vocabulary and how much it matters. The words we use have an influence on how we think, so watch what you say. I will give you a few examples. Avoid words like "don't", "won't", "can't", "no" and "problems". Don't say "I can't do this", "I will fail" or "I will lose my job". The subconscious mind cannot understand that negativity is bad for you and it cannot take a joke, so when you use negative words your mind will focus on them.

Think about *solutions* instead of problems. You can also focus on the *gifts* and *blessings* that are concealed in the problem and on *learning from problems.*

Furthermore, you can use words such as *prefer* or *choose* instead of "desire" or "want". For sample, *I have all the money I choose to have,* rather than "I have all the money I want." It makes you feel competent and in control. In the same way, instead of saying that you will "try", say that you *will.* It is also better to use the words *sometimes, often, usually,* instead of the more categorical "always" and "never".

Finally, remember that *I am, I can* and *I will* are powerful words indeed!

The poem below demonstrates that your attitude matters and that you can see things from different perspectives. When you change your perspective you see the same thing from a different angle. In other words, we see things through different lenses.

Attitude Determines Attitude
I woke up early today, excited over all I get to do before
the clock strikes midnight. I have responsibilities to
fulfill today. I am important. My job is to choose what
kind of day I am going to have.

Today I can complain because the weather is rainy, or I can be thankful that the grass is getting watered for free.

Today I can feel sad that I don't have more money, or I can be glad that my finances encourage me to plan my purchases wisely and guide me away from waste.

Today I can grumble about my health, or I can rejoice that I am alive.

Today I can lament over all that my parents didn't give me when I was growing up, or I can feel grateful that they allowed me to be born.

Today I can cry because roses have thorns, or I can celebrate that thorns have roses.

Today I can mourn my lack of friends, or I can excitedly embark upon a quest to discover new relationships.

Today I can whine because I have to go to work, or I can shout for joy because I have a job to do.

Today I can complain because I have to go to school, or eagerly open my mind and fill it with rich new tidbits of knowledge.

Today I can murmur dejectedly because I have to do housework, or I can feel honored because the Lord has provided shelter for my mind, body and soul.

Today stretches ahead of me, waiting to be shaped. And here I am, the sculptor who gets to do the shaping.

> What today will be like is up to me. I get to choose what
> kind of day I will have!
> Author unknown[7]

Values

Anything that changes your values changes your behavior.
George A. Sheehan

Values are those beliefs or ideals that are truly important to you. You have values whether or not you are aware of them. Your values influence your behaviour and attitude and serve as guidelines. In that way they can really help you. You may need to define your values in order to get to know who you are, as they are a central part of you. If you are not sure what your values are and would like to define them, you can start by looking back at your life. You can ask yourself questions such as:

- When was I happy? What was I doing and with whom?
- When was I satisfied and fulfilled? In what way? What activities or people made me feel satisfied and fulfilled?
- When was I proud of myself? What made me proud? What activities or people contributed to my feeling proud?

Values that were important to you in the past may not be relevant now or in the future. You might have to change your values in order to become who you would like to be. That is not easy but you can start by becoming aware of and reflecting on your values. You should also remember that if you continue to live according to the same values as previously, the outcome will be the same.

Ask yourself and reflect on the following question:

- What are my five main values? (For example, independence, joy, generosity, honesty, control.) Write them down.

Listing your five main values may be difficult. Try to determine what value you would choose in a certain situation if you had to choose just one. For example, if your two values are independence and control, which is the most important to you in a given situation?

Values can be deep or shallow. I have come across the following metaphor several times: Our deepest values are like glass balls. We do not want to drop them on the floor and risk breaking them. Less deeply held values are like rubber balls. We can choose to keep them in our hands or throw them and nothing much happens.

Values play a role when you make a big or small decision and also in how you treat other people. Your values influence your behaviour in general, so be careful with them because they can increase or decrease your joy of life.

Fear and Courage

The only thing we have to fear is fear itself.
Franklin D. Roosevelt

Fear has a huge influence on our lives and choices. By fear I mean self-doubt, worries and anxiety. We all have fears as fear is part of human nature. Fear and poor self-confidence are connected. Sometimes fear is totally unfounded. When we act in spite of fear it often turns out that what we feared was not as bad as we had imagined. Sometimes what you fear is external but it can also be a monster that you create yourself in your mind.

Most people prefer to remain for much of the time in their comfort zone, where they feel safe and comfortable, have the same thoughts as before and do the same things they have already done many times. There are no threats in the comfort zone and it is devoid of frightening experiences. It may be alarming to change and if you are afraid you are not alone! Fear is said to be our greatest enemy. You know what you have now but not what you will get in the future. Between reality and your dream there is fear.

However, most of the fear we try to avoid is exaggerated and in reality all that may happen when you battle your fear is that you learn something new.

The experience of embracing fear increases our strength and confidence. We can overcome fear if we acknowledge that we are afraid, try to look at the situation from different perspectives and take action regardless.

Instead of confronting fear, we often make excuses in order to avoid facing that which frightens us. This is because we consider fear something negative as opposed to positive. If you are afraid of failure you can change your way of looking at it, as there is no success without failure. The more you fail the closer you are to success. Remember that everyone who has succeeded in life has been afraid and overcome the fear. So can you!

Fear may also be a reason for procrastination, i.e., delaying or putting things off until the last possible moment. Are you good at finding excuses for not doing all those things you know that you should do and that would actually be very good for you to do? Then take a look at the examples below of common reasons for waiting, which may result in waiting until it is too late. Is this you?

> Until I have children, until my children leave home, until I lose 10 lbs, until I gain 10 lbs, until I have more money, until I get a divorce, until I get married, until next year, until I retire, until summer, until spring, until winter, until autumn.

There are many benefits of breaking the habit of delaying things. It will give you a relaxed feeling, a freedom of choice, so you can select your priorities and think about your next project in advance.

Try to identify what distractions are problematic, for example a need to check your e-mail or mobile phone for messages. Breaking down bigger tasks into smaller ones can enable you to place greater focus on every task. Giving yourself small rewards when you accomplish things may also help you to avoid procrastinating.

Another piece of advice is to make yourself feel good before you start doing what you have been putting off. Find something that you know will put you in a good mood.

Calling the fear something can decrease it. Maybe what you fear is something new and unknown and therefore you are afraid.

Fear can be good for you because it keeps you alert. Try to welcome the pain and fear when there is no way to escape it and remember, it will become easier once you start doing what you fear. It is the perception of it that may paralyze you the most.

Much of our fear originates from what we learnt when we were young. You learnt to be careful, that you can't do this or that and to be aware of what other people will think. However, just because people said things, it does not mean that they are true. The fears and doubts you have aren't even yours. You can let go of your fears and remind yourself that you are perfect as you are and that you don't need other people's approval.

A way to handle fear is to write it down. Draw two columns on a sheet of paper. Write plus above one of them and minus above the other. Write down the advantages and disadvantages of the change or challenge you are facing. Then write the positive and negative consequences of making the changes and not doing so. This may facilitate your decision-making process.

If you think that changes are difficult and challenging, what are you comparing them with? Remaining in a situation where you are not comfortable is no fun. What is more difficult, facing up to a challenge or remaining where you are?

When you are faced with a challenge, it is easy just to focus on risks. Is there any real risk or is it stepping out of the comfort zone that you fear? Remember all your previous challenges and fears. Did they change your life? Did you learn from them?

Ask yourself:

- When in my life have I faced fear and overcome it? What happened?
- When in my life have I faced fear and stopped myself? What happened?

One way of overcoming fear is to do what you are afraid of many times on a regular basis. This will make you feel relieved, proud of yourself and strengthen your self-confidence. For example, if you are afraid of speaking in front of a large group of people you can overcome much of your fear by doing it many times. I realized that when I obtained a lectureship at a university. You cannot be afraid of standing in front of students every day for many years! The fear and insecurity simply disappear over time.

Another good piece of advice when you are afraid of change is to take baby steps forward. Tiny steps are not frightening in the same way as big changes, yet you are changing. You could decide to do one little thing that frightens you every day.

A little fear or nervousness may be good for you in certain situations, such as speaking in public. You pull yourself together and concentrate on the task you are facing. Do you believe that you are more nervous about it than other speakers? This may have to do with comparing how you feel on the inside with how other people look on the outside.

Another way to cure fear is to obtain sufficient knowledge about the situation that causes fear. What do you fear? Failure? Rejection?

I remember a student I had some years ago who was very afraid of many things in his studies and life. I asked him if he feared failure or success. I still remember very clearly what an eye-opener that question was for him. He had never thought about the fact that he could fear success, only failure. How about you?

Why do we fear success? Doesn't it seem a bit stupid? Don't we all want to succeed? The fear of success is more widespread than you might think and there may be many reasons. You may fear the unknown or think that you do not deserve the consequences and rewards of success. You may fear success because you believe that it does not fit your own self-image or other people's image of you. You may fear success because you are afraid that other people will dislike it or envy you.

You may believe that you are not worthy of success or fear that the real you is stronger, more powerful and talented than you can handle. You may fear that you will be expected to perform at a higher level than before and face even greater challenges with the associated risk of falling flat on your face.

On the other hand, if you hold yourself back from success you diminish your true self and allow fear to control your life.

You may also fear making a mistake or a wrong decision or choice. But instead of using the word wrong you can look upon choices in another way, namely as good choices, the best or not the very best choices. In many cases you won't know until much later whether or not your choice was the best. However, you should bear in mind that you can always learn from a good or a less good choice.

When you feel frightened you are giving power to the fear. Fear, whether it is fear of failure, rejection or success, is so powerful that it can paralyze you. Don't let fear do that and conquer you! Ask yourself what you are afraid of: failure, rejection or success. Are you afraid of the feeling of failure, rejection or success or of its outcome?

A way of handling a challenge is to think about courage instead of fear. When you do something in spite of your fear you are courageous. The word courage comes from the Latin word "cor", meaning heart.

Courage is a habit you can learn through repetition, which implies facing the fear repeatedly. Courage is not the absence of fear but resistance to fear.

It takes courage to step out of your comfort zone and face risks and challenges, to think big and to feel an inner joy of life. You feel safe in the comfort zone. You strive for security instead of opportunity. You may also feel weak and helpless, considering that you are a victim of circumstances over which you have no control. Courage is not the absence of fear, it is the triumph over it, and reveals what you are truly capable of.

Courage enables you to face doubt and the criticism of other people. You can "train" your courage. The more often you are courageous and look fear in the face, the more courageous you will become. First of all you may have to give yourself permission to be courageous and look upon yourself as a courageous person.

One of the informants in my survey on joy of life mentioned daring more and how proud of or satisfied with herself she was when she did.

> ❖ *I want to dare more, get into more unproven situations, manage them and feel proud or satisfied.* (Woman, 70-79)

A way to encourage yourself to take risks is to plan to reward yourself. The reward does not have to be big or expensive. The important thing is that it makes the risk more attractive and your brain starts to desire that behaviour.

Worrying

> *There is no use worrying about things over which you have no control, and if you have control, you can do something about them instead of worrying.*
> Stanley C. Allyn

Do you worry a great deal? Then you are not alone! When I look back on my life and all the worrying I did, I come to the conclusion that most of the things I was worried about never happened. Remembering that helps me to worry far less today. I am sure you agree that wasting so much time worrying and causing yourself suffering is very stupid, especially as most of your worries are unfounded.

Worrying can be helpful when it makes you take action to solve problems or be more careful and avoid unnecessary risks. On the other hand, worry can be as paralyzing as fear and destroy both your day and your sleep at night. Worrying is also contagious, which means that you can make other people worry less or more. This implies that you should not spend much time with people who make you worry.

Melinda Smith, Robert Segal and Jeanne Segal[8] provide self-help on how to handle worrying. Here are a few of their tips:

- *Create a worry period.* You can learn to postpone worrying by creating a "worry period" consisting of a defined amount of time, such as 30 minutes or whatever you consider suitable. It should be at the same time every day and not close to bedtime. When worrying thoughts arise postpone them until your worry period. You may have to make a list in order to feel certain that you will not forget about what to think about during your worry period. This will make you realize that you have more control over your worrying than you think.

- *Ask yourself if the problem is solvable or unsolvable.* If the worry is solvable, make a list of possible solutions. After evaluating your options, make a plan of action. If the worry is about something that you cannot solve, you must try to accept uncertainty.

This last tip is similar to the so-called Serenity Prayer: God grant me the serenity to accept the things I cannot change, the courage to change the things I can, and the wisdom to know the difference.

Here is a third tip:

- *Challenge anxious thoughts.* Start by identifying your frightening thoughts and ask yourself if there are more realistic and positive ways of looking at the problem. Are you looking at things in black and white categories? Are you over-generalizing, diminishing the positive sides, jumping to conclusions without evidence, expecting the worst-case scenario, too hard to yourself about what you should and should not do and assuming responsibility for things that are beyond your control?

What may also help you to worry less is spending more time in the present. Living in the moment relaxes us. In addition, try to activate yourself by doing things that prevent you from dwelling on your worries.

Before I let you relax with a little story, I would like to add something that I have experienced many times when I have been worried. Not only did things turn out differently to what I expected, meaning that I had worried for no reason, but I frequently did not know until later whether the outcome was to my advantage.

Here is a story about a wise man telling a young boy his life secret.

Think, Believe, Dream and Dare
An eight year old boy approached an old man in front of a wishing well, looked up into his eyes, and asked: "I understand you're a very wise man. I'd like to know the secret of life."

The old man looked down at the youngster and replied: "I've thought a lot in my lifetime, and the secret can be summed up in four words.

The first is think. Think about the values you wish to live your life by.

The second is believe. Believe in yourself based on the thinking you've done about the values you're going to live your life by.

The third is dream. Dream about the things that can be, based on your belief in yourself and the values you're going to live by.

The last is dare. Dare to make your dreams become reality, based on your belief in yourself and your values."

And with that, Walter E. Disney said to the little boy: "Think, Believe, Dream, and Dare."[9]

KEY 3: GRATITUDE

Gratitude helps you to grow and expand; gratitude brings joy and laughter into your life and into the lives of all those around you.
Eileen Caddy

Gratitude is maybe the most important key to joy of life. Being grateful for what we have increases our feeling of well-being and makes us more optimistic. Gratitude empowers us.

In his article "Why gratitude is good"[1] Robert A. Emmons, who is an expert on gratitude and has studied its effects on physical health, psychological well-being and our relationships with other people, stated that gratitude is good for our body, mind and relationships. Here are some likely benefits of gratitude:

Physical
You will
- have a stronger immune system
- be less bothered by aches and pain
- have lower blood pressure
- exercise more and take better care of your health
- sleep longer and feel more refreshed on waking

Psychological
You will
- have a higher level of positive emotions
- be more alert, alive and awake
- experience more joy and pleasure
- be more optimistic and happier

Social
You will
- be more helpful, generous and compassionate
- be more forgiving
- be more outgoing
- feel less lonely and isolated

Emmons states that his definition of gratitude has two components: "It's an affirmation of goodness. We affirm that there are good things in the world, gifts and benefits we have received. This does not mean that life is perfect; it does not ignore complaints, burdens, and hassles." According to Emmons, the second part of gratitude concerns "figuring out where that goodness comes from. We recognize the sources of this goodness as being outside of ourselves....We acknowledge that other people gave us many gifts, big and small, to help us achieve the goodness in our lives."

Emmons considers that there are many important reasons why gratitude may have such transformative effects on people's lives. Here are four of them:

Firstly, *gratitude allows us to celebrate the present,* which means that we appreciate the value of something and are less likely to take it for granted. Secondly, *gratitude blocks toxic, negative emotions* such as envy, resentment and regret. You cannot feel envious and grateful at the same time. Thirdly, *grateful people are more stress resistant.* Fourthly, *grateful people have a higher sense of self-worth.* Once you have become aware of your own value, you can transform the way you see yourself.

Gratitude is not always easy. There is that "self-serving bias", i.e., when good things happen to us we say it is because of something we did and when bad things happen we blame others or circumstances. This contradicts gratitude because when we are grateful we give credit to other people for our success.

Gratitude also goes against our need to feel in control. We have to accept life as it is and be grateful for what we have. Furthermore, it contradicts the idea that bad things happen to good people and vice versa. Gratitude makes us realize that we have more than we deserve.

How can you become a more grateful person? Emmons recommends keeping a gratitude journal, which means listing just five things every week for which we are grateful. It also guards against taking things for granted. Another strategy is to count your blessings regularly, in the morning or in the evening.

It is important to think outside of the box. In his book *Thanks! How Practicing Gratitude Can Make You Happier*[2] Emmons mentions Mother Teresa, who talked about how grateful she was to the sick and dying people she helped in the slums of Calcutta, because they made it possible for her to grow and deepen her compassion. That is an example of thinking about gratitude as something we can give as opposed to receive.

In another article by Emmons[3], "How Gratitude Can Help You Through Hard Times", he talks about how essential it is to have a grateful attitude to and perspective on life, especially in difficult times.

Gratitude has the power to heal and bring hope. Emmons points out that it is vital to make a distinction between feeling grateful and being grateful. Feeling grateful comes from the way we look at the world whereas being grateful is a choice. It is an attitude that is not easily affected by the gains and losses that flow in and out of our lives. Gratitude gives us a perspective from which we can view life as a whole when we risk being overwhelmed by temporary circumstances.

When times are good we take many things for granted, so a crisis may help us to be more grateful but gratitude can also help us cope with a crisis. Gratitude builds a kind of psychological immune system and research shows that grateful people are more resilient to stress.

Emmons suggests that you should think of the worst times in your life and then remember that you are here now and that you endured them. Contrasting the present with bad times in the past can make you feel less unhappy and improve your sense of well-being.

Another way of helping you to be grateful is, according to Emmons, to confront your own mortality. In a study, researchers asked participants to imagine a scenario in which they died due to being trapped in a burning skyscraper. The result revealed that the gratitude levels of the intervention group members increased when compared with a control group, the members of which were not asked to imagine their own death. We can compare this finding with what may happen when someone survives a disease, such as lung cancer, as described in the Introduction.

Emmons suggests that you can try to change how you think about some past unpleasant experience using the language of thankfulness. Whether it was a large or a small event, asking yourself questions such as the following can help you:

- What lessons did the experience teach me?
- Can I find ways to be thankful for what happened to me now, even though I was not at the time it happened?
- Have my negative feelings about the experience limited or prevented me from feeling gratitude since it occurred?

The goal of such questions is to gain a new perspective on the experience, not to relive it.

Here are some more reasons why gratitude is good from Emmons' article:

- Grateful people have 10% fewer stress related illnesses, are more physically fit and have lower blood pressure.
- Gratitude is related to age: For every ten years, gratitude increases by 5%.
- Overall positive emotions can add up to seven years to your life.

- Grateful people have more satisfying relationships with others, and are better liked.

The effects of gratitude are very impressive! Don't you agree? In another article, "10 Ways to Become More Grateful"[4], Robert Emmons provides tips for living a life of gratitude, some of which I have already mentioned. Here is a summary of them:

1. *Keep a Gratitude Journal.* Establish a daily practice in which you remind yourself of the gifts, grace, benefits and good things to enjoy.
2. *Remember the Bad.* By remembering how difficult life was and how far you have come, you highlight the contrast in your mind, which facilitates gratefulness.
3. *Use Visual Reminders.* You might need visual reminders to trigger thoughts of gratitude. The best visual reminders are other people.
4. *Watch your Language.* Grateful people use words like gifts, giver, blessings, blessed, fortunate and abundance.
5. *Go Through the Motions.* Grateful motions include smiling, saying thank you and writing letters to express one's gratitude.
6. *Think Outside the Box.* Look for new situations and circumstances in which to feel grateful.

Read the following if you still experience difficulty finding things to be grateful for:

Are You Blessed?
If you wake up this morning with more health than illness....you are more blessed than the million who will not survive this week.

If you have never experienced the danger of battle, the loneliness of imprisonment, the agony of torture, or the pangs of starvation.......you are ahead of 500 million people in the world.

If you have food in the refrigerator, clothes on your back, a roof overhead and a place to sleep...you are richer than 75% of this world.

If you have money in the bank, in your wallet, and spare change in a dish someplace....... you are among the top 8% of the world's wealthy.

If you hold up your head with a smile on your face and are truly thankful.....you are blessed because the majority can, but most do not.

If you can read now, you are more blessed than over two billion people in the world who cannot read at all.
Author unknown[5]

Amie M. Gordon[6] published an article entitled "Five Ways Giving Thanks Can Backfire", in which she confirms that most of the time gratitude is good for your health, well-being and relationships. However, research results also reveal situations when "thank you" may be the wrong response. For example, you can overdose on gratitude by focusing on quantity over quality. You may use gratitude to avoid a serious problem or downplay your own success by letting gratitude get in the way of taking credit for your part in success. You can also mistake gratitude for indebtedness and thus try to take the weight of a debt off your shoulders.

I think that there is a bigger risk of not being sufficiently grateful than of being too grateful. One reason may be that we forget to thank people who have done us a favour or given us a gift, invited us to dinner or sent a postcard or Christmas card.

From my mother I learnt how important it is never to forget to confirm the receipt of a gift, especially one sent by post. "I want to know that it has arrived" she used to say. But that is not the only reason for remembering to express your thanks for a gift or card. Saying thank you is a way of practicing gratefulness and showing respect to people who have done something for you. We all have a need to be seen and appreciated and saying thanks fulfils that need. Feeling appreciated is said to be our greatest emotional need and is oxygen for the mind.

In my experience, younger generations today, at least in Europe, seem to take expressing thanks less seriously or are inclined to forget it. Of course that is not the case with all younger people, but with some people I have met it seems to be a trend that may be a result of new ways of communicating and new technology. Whatever the reason, I think it is a great pity because saying thank you is very rewarding for both parties.

We are all reminded now and then of the importance of living in the present, carpe diem. It does not mean that we have to be happy all the time. Nobody is. Some days are more difficult than others. We fall ill, people close to us fall ill or die. Daily life is full of large or small problems to be solved, in addition to coping with disappointments and failures. These things happen in the outer world. However, if you experience gratefulness and an inner joy of life that is not derived from what happens in the outer world but is an attitude, you can better cope with the hardships of life.

Nevertheless, being grateful does not mean that you should settle for less than you deserve or desire.

Being grateful is a choice that can improve many important aspects of your life such as health and joy of life, your way of coping with daily challenges and make you more positive. You will find that when you stop taking so many things for granted and instead focus on feeling grateful, there will be so much more to be grateful for.

Here are some pieces of advice and questions to reflect on:

- o Observe your thoughts. Are your thoughts positive, negative, or appreciative?
- o Do you think of gifts or problems?
- o Say the two words "Thank you" as often as you can.
- o Tell people you are grateful when you are, as it will increase both your own and their joy of life.

Count your blessings. You can do that in various ways including the gratitude journal I have already mentioned. Here are some further examples:

- o Write down what has enriched your day every evening.
- o Start thinking of people who have expressed their gratitude to you and remember people who have been happy because you were in their lives.

- Think of what you have and you will feel joy instead of regretting what you don't have, which will make you feel sad.

You can also reflect on how important it is to forget occasions when people have hurt you and instead recall when they did something good for you. Here is a story about that:

Sand and Stone
Two friends were walking through the desert. At one point of the journey they had an argument, and one friend slapped the other in the face. The one who got slapped was hurt, but without saying anything wrote in the sand: "TODAY MY BEST FRIEND SLAPPED ME IN THE FACE."

They kept on walking until they found an oasis, where they decided to take a bath. The one who had been slapped got stuck in the mire and started drowning, but the other saved him. After the friend recovered from the near drowning, he wrote on a stone: "TODAY MY BEST FRIEND SAVED MY LIFE."

The one who had slapped and then saved his best friend asked him, "After I hurt you, you wrote in the sand. Now, you write on a stone. Why?"

The other friend replied: "When someone hurts us, we should write it down in sand where winds of forgiveness can erase it. But, when someone does something good for us we must engrave it in stone where no wind can ever erase it."

Learn to write your hurts in the sand and to carve your blessings in stone.

Author unknown[7]

In his article "Pay it Forward" Robert Emmons[8] tells us about Elisabeth Bartlett, a professor of political science, who developed a life-threatening heart disease at the age of 42 for which a heart transplant was the only hope. She was fortunate and received one. She described being thankful for her new life but also that simply feeling thankful was not enough.

She had a desire to do something in return, to give thanks, things, thoughts, love and not only to the donor but to whoever crossed her path. Gratitude became something more than a pleasant feeling; it was also motivating. It moved her to share and increase the good she had received.

Gratitude makes us aware of our dependence on others and we feel obliged to reciprocate. According to Emmons, research has shown that grateful people offer others more emotional support or help. In this way gratitude motivates people to do good.

I don't know if you recognize this feeling of motivation to do good yourself. I do. I experienced it very strongly after I had survived lung cancer. But that was not the only time, as I also remember how grateful I was many years ago when a colleague helped me in a very generous way to access opportunities that had an enormous impact on my future career. I realized that I would never be able to pay him back or thank him enough. Instead, I concentrated on generously giving my students more of my time and effort.

I don't know if that was the reason I received so many presents, flowers, thank you cards and e-mails from students. However, I remember how happy I was to receive all those gifts and other expressions of appreciation.

One of the many examples of my students' gratitude occurred a few days before Christmas, when a wonderful class of 30 students gave me a huge basket full of fruit, wine and Christmas food just before the break. I was overwhelmed and told them that no student was allowed to leave the class room before I had given her/him a hug. A few days later I came down with the flu and was ill for the whole of the Christmas holidays. Nevertheless, despite my strong suspicion that it could have been caused by the hugs, I still remember with joy those wonderful students and that basket!

Below is an example of how gratefulness can have an astonishing effect many years later.

Paid in full with one glass of milk

One day, a poor boy who was selling goods from door to door to pay his way through school, found he had only one thin dime left, and he was hungry. He decided he would ask for a meal at the next house.

However, he lost his nerve when a lovely young woman opened the door. Instead of a meal he asked for a drink of water. She thought he looked hungry so brought him a large glass of milk.

He drank it slowly, and then asked, "How much do I owe you?"

"You don't owe me anything," she replied. "Mother has taught us never to accept pay for a kindness."

He said, "Then I thank you from my heart."

As Howard Kelly left that house, he not only felt stronger physically, but his faith in God and man was strong also. He had been ready to give up and quit.

Years later that young woman became critically ill. The local doctors were baffled. They finally sent her to the big city, where they called in specialists to study her rare disease.

Dr. Howard Kelly was called in for the consultation. When he heard the name of the town she came from, a strange light filled his eyes. Immediately he rose and went down the hall of the hospital to her room.

Dressed in his doctor's gown he went in to see her. He recognized her at once. He went back to the consultation room determined to do his best to save her life. From that day he gave special attention to the case.

After a long struggle, the battle was won. Dr. Kelly requested the business office to pass the final bill to him for approval. He looked at it, then wrote something on the edge and the bill was sent to her room.

She feared to open it, for she was sure it would take the rest of her life to pay for it all. Finally she looked, and something caught her attention on the side of the bill. She began to read the following words:

"*Paid in full with one glass of milk.*
Signed, Dr. Howard Kelly."

Author Unknown[9]

In his article "Pay it Forward"[10], Emmons also shows through his research that people who are grateful get more hours of sleep each night. They spend less time awake before falling asleep and feel more refreshed upon wakening. Emmons suggests that if you want to sleep more soundly, you should count blessings, not sheep!

Maybe you agree with all this in theory and find gratitude wonderful. But how can you be grateful if you are having a very hard time at present or are depressed and feel that life just is not fair?

Victoria Maxwell[11], who had bi-polar disorder, described how difficult it can be to be grateful in the midst of depression. She said that gratitude "had not been in the picture." Even when she wasn't depressed she had a difficult time with gratitude. However, she recently became aware of her blessings and started to ask herself what gratitude means to her. Here are some of her tips for practicing gratitude when you feel down.

1. Close your eyes. Sit somewhere when you have time on your own.
2. Take a deep breath.
3. Say or visualize the word gratitude in your mind.
4. Focus on your body.
5. Breathe a little deeper and relax.
6. Mentally review things, occurrences and people you have experienced in the last 24 hours, as well as during the last week or two. Ask yourself for what or whom you feel gratitude. Vulnerability is one reason why feeling gratitude can be frightening and thus avoided. Envy, jealousy and bitterness are other reasons.
7. When you discover something that gives you a sense of gratitude, observe what it is like.
8. Take a deep breath and open your eyes. Give yourself a pat on the back.

Does this work for you? If so, do it again and again!

A way to help yourself learn and practice gratitude may be to reflect on or write about a person or situation that does not please you. Try to determine what you learnt from that person or situation and express your gratitude for that learning.

I will end this chapter with a story that can be seen as a summary of some of the things I wanted to tell you about gratitude.

Heart of Gratitude
A blind boy sat on the steps of a building with a hat by his feet. He held up a sign which said: 'I am blind, please help.' There were only a few coins in the hat.

A man was walking by. He took a few coins from his pocket and dropped them into the hat. He then took the sign, turned it around, and wrote some words. He put the sign back so that everyone who walked by would see the new words.

Soon the hat began to fill up. A lot more people were giving money to the blind boy. That afternoon the man who had changed the sign came to see how things were. The boy recognized his footsteps and asked, "Were you the one who changed my sign this morning? What did you write?" The man said, "I only wrote the truth. I said what you said but in a different way. I wrote: 'Today is a beautiful day but I cannot see it.'"

Both signs told people that the boy was blind. But the first sign simply said the boy was blind. The second sign told people that they were so lucky that they were not blind. Should we be surprised that the second sign was more effective?

Be thankful for what you have. Be creative. Be innovative. Think differently and positively.

  Enjoy your day with a heart of gratitude.
                    Author unknown[12]

KEY 4: FORGIVENESS

> *Forgiveness has nothing to do with absolving a criminal of his crime. It has everything to do with relieving oneself of the burden of being a victim – letting go of the pain and transforming oneself from victim to survivor.*
> Alison Croggon

For a long time I have been so impressed when I learn about people who have forgiven really difficult offences, which does not mean that I think it is easy to forgive minor offences either. How did they manage to forgive in South Africa? How can people in Cambodia or Rwanda forgive all those murders? How can Holocaust survivors forgive? How can people who have experienced the horrors of war all over the planet ever forgive?

These are some examples of extremely difficult experiences that people try to forgive and actually succeed. Hopefully, you have less difficult experiences to forgive but it may still not be easy. The above mentioned examples concern public apologies and involve many people. In this chapter I am going to mainly discuss private apologies between individuals, where both the offender and the offended are easy to identify.

Have you ever experienced how neighbours, relatives or friends become really bogged down by a conflict or grudge? So bogged down that they stop talking to each other? I have! Have you ever thought about what a waste that is when instead they could enjoy wonderful relationships and communication? Or couldn't they at least try to be friendly and polite to each other? But they are unable to do so because they are hurt, humiliated and keep blaming the other party in the conflict, thinking that as she/he does not say Hello to me I can't say Hello to her/him. Did the conflict seem unnecessary, trivial and resolvable to you? Isn't life too short to waste time on having hard feelings about people you used to like?

I am sure you agree with me on this, yet this situation happens around us all the time. So, what about you? Do you also find it difficult to forgive? I think we all experience difficulties asking for forgiveness and forgiving. Letting go of the grudge for a moment and being the one who says Hello to your adversary despite believing that everything is her/his fault should be fairly easy, but in fact it is not.

A grudge is based on anger and humiliation. You feel powerless. I personally believe that humiliating a person is one of the worst things you can do. Maybe you don't want to admit to being humiliated but you are and when that happens you may start thinking of revenge.

I remember an incident at work many years ago when I had finished for the day and was rushing to collect my children from pre-school. I was already late when I met my boss on the stairs on my way out. He ordered me in an unfriendly and resolute voice to return to my office because he needed me to send an important telex. I became very upset but did as I was told. My boss watched me sitting there by the telex machine with my coat on and with tears running down my cheeks.

That whole evening I felt very upset, angry and humiliated and thought about revenge. At first I did not know what to do but before I fell asleep that night I had a plan. The next morning at work I phoned my boss and said I was sorry and asked him to forgive me for my bad behaviour. That was not what he had expected! The result was that he apologized too and said he was so sorry because he realized that as a single mother I had more things to take responsibility for than my work.

Neither of us had intended to apologise but when I did, I felt that I regained control. I was proud of my initiative, despite the fact that the aim had been to take revenge by showing my strength and make him feel ashamed. After that day there were no hard feelings between us. He had learnt a lesson and so had I. There is no doubt that this was an important event for me as I still remember it very clearly after so many years.

In his article "Research on the science of forgiveness" Adam Cohen[1] states that until a few years ago forgiveness did not receive much attention from psychologists but then researchers began to focus on what forgiveness is and whether it is healthy. According to Cohen, defining it has turned out to be a challenge. Is it an emotion or a behaviour? The researchers Julia Juola Exline and Roy Baumeister (referred to in Cohen's article) came to the conclusion that forgiveness can be both.

What does it mean to forgive? First of all, it is impossible to avoid hurts and disappointments but according to Fred Luskin[2], you have a choice in how you react to and handle them. Forgiveness can help you to repair a damaged relationship but does not oblige you to reconcile with the person who harmed you, as it has nothing to do with justice. Forgiveness is not denying the seriousness of an offence and does not mean forgetting or excusing offences. You forgive for your own sake to release yourself from guilt and shame. Forgiveness is not for the other person, it is for you. You can also forgive yourself, to which I will return later.

Forgiveness brings peace of mind to the person who forgives and can help her/him let go of anger. It also enables her/him to heal and move on with life.

Thus, if you don't forgive, what hurts you may become an obstacle in your life, which is bad enough but there is more. People close to you, such as your partner, parents or colleagues may also suffer when you hold a grudge against someone. There is even a risk of passing on your anger, hatred, hurt and bitterness to your children and grandchildren. Ask yourself if it is really worth it!

Fred Luskin[3] suggests nine steps to forgiveness. Some of them are about articulating what is not OK about the situation and making a commitment to yourself to feel better as forgiveness is for you and no one else. It is about gaining the right perspective on what happened. It is also important to recognize that your distress is due to your feelings and thoughts, not what offended or hurt you.

Another step is to remember the adage that a life well lived may be your best revenge. In my view this can be very true in some situations, for example after a divorce, a cheating spouse or when you lose your job. This was an eye-opener for me when I first learnt about it a few years ago and several times I have seen how true it can be. Instead of focusing on your hurt feelings and thereby giving power to the person who caused you pain, you should focus on how to improve yourself and your own life. Look for the beauty and kindness around you. Devote more energy to appreciating what you have instead of what you do not have.

It may take courage to ask for forgiveness and you may be reluctant for many reasons. Sometimes it may feel easier to do it by writing a letter, an e-mail or a text.

If you cannot say the words "I am sorry" or "Please, forgive me" you can start by being more kind, generous and respectful towards the person. In the long run it is difficult to resist kindness, generosity and respect. Perhaps you can ask the person to forgive you at a later stage when the timing feels more appropriate. When you want to learn to forgive you can start by forgiving minor offences.

Luskin[4] says that forgiving is being resilient when things don't go the way you want, being at peace with what is and with the vulnerability inherent in human life. Forgiveness is grief. When you are offended or hurt grief is a normal response/reaction and forgiveness resolves grief, helping you to let go of your suffering and move on.

If you have hurt somebody and need to be forgiven, you will be more likely to receive forgiveness if the person you have hurt can see the distress or remorse you feel for having hurt her/him.

Jack Kornfield[5] explains that forgiveness is the capacity to let go, release the suffering and choose the mystery of love instead. Kornfield cites the Bhagavad Gita: "If you want to see the brave, look to those who can return love for hatred. If you want to see the heroic, look to those who can forgive."

Kornfield reminds us that it is not necessary to be loyal to your suffering. We are very loyal to our suffering, focusing on the trauma and betrayal of "what happened to me". Yes, it happened and it was terrible! But is that what defines you?

Furthermore, Kornfield adds that it is not worth living with hatred day after day. "Because for one thing, that person who betrayed you could be in Hawaii right now having a nice vacation – and you're here hating them! Who's suffering then?"

Here is another way of expressing more or less the same point:

Having resentment against someone is like drinking poison and thinking it will kill your enemy.
Nelson Mandela

Kornfield declares that forgiveness is not sentimental, or quick. It is a process that can take a long time, as you have to deal with your grief, anger, hurt and fear.

He relates a story about a young boy that I will retell below.

Killing the Murderer

The boy was 14 years old when he shot a kid as an initiation rite in order to join a gang. At the end of the trial where he was convicted of murder, the mother of the shot kid stood up, looked him in the eye and said: "I am going to kill you."

After some years this mother started to visit the convicted boy in prison, talking to him, giving him a little money and other things he needed. When he was about to be released from prison the mother of the shot kid asked him "What are you going to do?" He answered that he had no idea because he had no family, nothing. She then helped him to get a job in a factory.

She asked him where he was going to stay and got the same answer. He did not know and she told him that she had a spare room where he could stay with her. One day about six months later she told him she needed to talk with him. She asked him if he remembered that day in court when he was convicted of murdering her son and she had said that she would kill him. He remembered that very well. Then she said: "Well I have." She explained that she did not want a boy who could kill in cold blood like that to continue to exist in the world. So she set about changing him and now he was not the same person any more. She asked him if she could adopt him because she did not have anybody and she needed a son. He said "Yes!" and so she did.

You can ask yourself what benefits you can gain from bad and painful experiences of being hurt. Did they change your life in any way? Can you now admit that what happened actually changed your life in a positive way? It might have changed you as a person and altered your circumstances. Maybe you moved, changed jobs or got divorced because of what happened and that turned out to be one of the best things that happened in your life. Maybe you decided never to treat anybody like you were treated and it helped you become a better person. When you think about it, what happened might even be a misunderstanding or caused by the fact that you or the other person just did not understand.

People do what they do because of their goals, priorities, rationales, beliefs and values, so in reality their attacks may have had nothing whatsoever to do with you. The world does not revolve around you. People do not think about you as much as you may believe they do. So, avoid taking everything that happened to you personally. In reality you may have just happened to be that person's nearest punching bag!

When you feel victimized and play the victim you may experience how the grudge runs in your head like a film over and over again. This is very energy consuming and prevents you from using your energy for better purposes.

We feel guilty and ashamed when we believe that we are causing other people pain. We judge what we do, think, say or feel to be bad. Often children feel guilty because they think that their behaviour or actions are causing pain to their parents or siblings. This can continue to have an effect on us when we are adults without us being aware of it. It can turn into limiting beliefs and act as a barrier. Blaming yourself may also result in stress, depression and addiction.

Another way of dealing with your mistakes and wrongdoings is to just accept what happened without judgment, guilt or shame. Acceptance and forgiveness will help you to gain more energy and facilitate healing.

Sonia Choquette[6] writes about the power of forgiveness and states that nothing can sabotage your ability to be alert, awake and fully present in the moment as much as being resentful of or holding a grudge against someone. It is important that you can look in the mirror and be proud of the person you see there.

She says:

> If you are mentally or emotionally consumed by the negative energy of a past injury, over 90% of our awareness will be distracted from the moment, because it's engaged with nursing your wounds from the past. Not only does carrying resentment from the past rob you of all ability to be fully present, it also causes you to shield yourself from future abuses by constructing defensive walls around you.

An example of defensive walls is when you were hurt in a love relationship, which resulted in you putting a defensive wall or "a barbed wire fence around your heart" as Kellie Pickler sings. Thus you do not allow yourself to be vulnerable but if you keep the wall or barbed wire fence around your heart for long you cannot move on and may miss out on new relationships.

According to Sonia Choquette, the first and best way to forgive, forget and move on is to objectively examine what happened. Sometimes you may need to stop yourself from taking the things done to you personally.

Sonia Choquette suggests some reasons to forgive. According to her, forgiveness is good for your health and can increase your life expectancy. It may heighten your awareness and intuition and improve your energy. It may also attract people to you and make life easier for you and the people around you as it lifts your heart and creates positive vibes. In addition, it can sharpen your creativity.

Sonia Choquette also suggests that in order to forgive you should not blame yourself for mistakes but take responsibility for your part in upset and injury. Claim the gifts hidden in perceived injuries and see all events as opportunities to grow and mature. Forgive yourself and count your blessings. Develop a sense of humour and talk about today's positive events instead of past injuries.

Researchers have been interested in whether it is healthy to forgive. This question and its answer are important for those who want to choose more joy in their life, as good health helps you to experience more joy. According to Luskin[7], forgiveness can reduce stress, blood pressure, anger and hurt, as well as increasing physical vitality.

Loren Tuossaint and Jon R. Webb[8] state that studies have revealed a connection between forgiveness and physical, mental and spiritual health and that forgiveness plays a key role in the health of families, communities and nations.

Cohen[9] asks whether forgiveness is possible and healthy in extreme cases, such as genocide and refers to the researchers Ervin Staub and Laurie Anne Pearlman, who came to the conclusion that forgiving is also necessary and desirable in these cases, as they believe that forgiveness paves the way to reconditioning and healing, as well as promoting psychological well-being.

However, there are different opinions on the question of whether certain things are unforgivable. According to Jason March[10], some researchers suggest that forgiveness is necessary to promote healing and well-being, even after acts such as murder or genocide but in such difficult cases a period of time, for example six months, should be allowed to pass first.

Do women apologise more often than men? Yes, according to Lazare[11] they do. They are more comfortable in admitting their vulnerability. However, the previously mentioned study by Loren Toussaint and Jon R. Webb[12] demonstrated that while women were more empathetic than men, no gender difference in relation to forgiveness was apparent.

Is it easier for older people to forgive? I think it might be. Our view of what is important changes with advancing age. We also realize more than ever that if we postpone an apology it may be too late. Time is running out for us and other older people in our lives.

What is the difference between receiving an apology and being forgiven? In his book *On Apology* Aron Lazare[13] defines the concept of apology:

> Apology refers to an encounter between two parties in which one party, the offender, acknowledges responsibility for an offence or grievance and expresses regret or remorse to a second party, the aggrieved.

According to Lazare, forgiveness means that you feel released from guilt and shame. It's about and for you. An apology, on the other hand, means that two parties, the offender and the aggrieved, risk being uncomfortable or hurt. The apology can fail. Forgiveness may happen without an apology. However, there is no guarantee that an apology will result in forgiveness. There may be no forgiveness in spite of an apology.

Lazare points out that the most essential part of an effective apology is acknowledging the offence. It is also important that the offender exhibits remorse, i.e., deep regret for what she/he did wrong and for causing pain. It is necessary to understand the offence from the perspective of the offended person. To be successful an apology must meet one or more of the psychological needs of the aggrieved party. Examples are restoring self-respect, ensuring that the two parties have shared values and seeing that the offender has suffered as a result of the offence.

To admit that you made a mistake, feel remorse and perhaps shame requires acting with humility and serenity. You want the aggrieved person to trust you again but trust cannot be built without demonstrating that you are sincere. If you have lied, you have to stop immediately, admit it and show that you are still worthy of trust. If the consequences of your offence and lies are severe, you may have a chance to learn from them and become a person who does not lie.

There are many more gains in the process. If you are looking for more joy of life you can think about gratefulness and look for the gift in the sad event. One gift may be what you learn from it all. Another can be that your attitude or values change. You can rid yourself of limiting beliefs, for example you can change from blaming yourself for being weak and fearful to experiencing the courage needed to ask for forgiveness or to forgive.

Sometimes you are not aware that you have hurt another person. Here is an example.

Many years ago I felt offended and humiliated by a colleague. In my view he had acted in a way that was certainly not OK with me. He assumed that he had the right to change the rules in an area in which I was very experienced and competent, without consulting me. I felt humiliated, powerless and disappointed as I had always liked this colleague very much. I told him that I had never ever been treated by anyone with so much lack of respect.

After that I did not see him for about two weeks and when we suddenly bumped into one another I realized that I had hurt him! I was very surprised because it had never occurred to me that he could be hurt by what I had said about lack of respect. All I thought about during those two weeks was that I had been hurt. When I understood the whole situation, all I could think of to say was "I'm sorry". He repeated the same to me and after that we were on speaking terms. However, our previous very friendly and happy work relationship never returned completely.

My conclusion is that we both failed to meet the other's psychological needs, for example ensuring that we had similar values.

> *True forgiveness is when you can say, "Thank you for the experience!"*
> Oprah Winfrey

Forgiving Yourself

> *The weak can never forgive. Forgiveness is the attribute of the strong.*
> Mahatma Gandhi.

What did Mahatma Gandhi mean by the above quotation? I think he meant that it takes a strong mind to forgive. The weak are unable to let go of anger or the need for revenge and payback. The weak tend to hold on to their hurt feelings. It's the same with forgiving yourself. You can look upon forgiveness as the best gift you can give to yourself and others, but you have to be strong to be able to forgive yourself.

According to Juliana Breines[14], forgiving yourself can help to free you from unpleasant feelings such as guilt and shame, but there is also a risk that it can reduce your empathy for others and the motivation to make amends because it can provide you with a sense of moral righteousness as opposed to moral responsibility.

While this may be true, I nevertheless believe that when it comes to forgiveness, the advantages are generally far greater than the risks.

Breines stresses that self-forgiveness is a slow process and the result is not all or nothing. It may never result in a full release of negative feelings. In order to forgive yourself you must admit to yourself that what you did was wrong and that you deserve to be forgiven. It can help you eliminate the anger towards yourself and accept who you are.

A friend of mine told me about her mother who died a few years ago at the age of 89. During her mother's last two years she lived in a retirement home. My friend went to see her every week and they talked and laughed and enjoyed each other's company. But sometimes her mother became confused and told stories she believed had happened but for obvious reasons could not be true.

One day when my friend went to visit her mother she found that her mother was angry and accused her of having abandoned her mother when they went for a walk on the beach two days earlier. The mother said that they had had a good time together until the daughter suddenly ran away and did not come back. The mother claimed that she had had to spend the whole night on the beach until she was found early in the morning by a man walking his dog, who helped her back to the retirement home.

When my friend heard this she became very angry and told her mother to stop fantasizing. It was untrue that they had gone to the beach as there was no beach near the retirement home and if they had been to a beach my friend would never have abandoned her mother. Besides, the mother could barely walk indoors with a walker, so for her a walk on the beach was just impossible. However, the mother insisted that it was true and my friend was now so angry that she started to scream at her mother and left in anger.

That night the mother suffered a heart attack and died! Now my friend felt so guilty for screaming at her mother. She realized that she had acted wrongly because her mother could not help having difficulties differentiating between what was reality and fantasies or bad dreams. What could she do now to forgive herself and to obtain her mother's forgiveness? She told me that her way of handling this situation was to write a letter to her mother and ask for forgiveness. She then put the letter among other letters and keepsakes in a box. After writing the letter she was able to let go and forgive herself, which alleviated her guilt to some extent.

When I was writing this chapter on forgiveness I felt pleased with myself because I recalled that during the last few years I had struggled to forgive people who are important to me and was happy to note that I had more or less succeeded in doing so.

Then something happened. Memories came to my mind that I did not want to think about because they were still painful after many, many years. I realized that I may have forgiven others but had not forgiven myself for behaving very selfishly in certain situations when I was young! And I also realized that I still avoided similar situations. The experience had resulted in the limiting belief that in certain situations I am very selfish. That is how I am and it cannot be changed! All I could do was to avoid such situations for the rest of my life, which is what I did. I had had that limiting belief for a very long time and no doubt it held me back!

This was indeed a very interesting discovery. Now I had a chance to practice what I was writing about. I stopped writing for a few days and thought a great deal about what had happened long ago, reflecting on the circumstances. Maybe it was not my fault after all. Perhaps the circumstances combined with my being young and immature made me act in a seemingly selfish way. Maybe I would act differently today, if I just had the courage to expose myself to a similar situation. Perhaps I am not such a selfish person after all!

However, when I looked back on my life, I realized that there were other situations that had nothing to do with my being young, where I had acted in a selfish way. I wondered: Aren't we all selfish at some times in our lives? What is selfishness? I realized that selfishness mainly comes from feelings of insecurity and fear. When we change and grow within ourselves, when we become more confident and safe, our selfishness decreases. The opportunity to reflect on this was a big eye-opener for me, for which I am now very grateful.

What about you? What things have you not forgiven yourself for? Ask yourself the following questions:

- What situations do I avoid and could a reason be that I have not forgiven myself?

- Are there any limiting beliefs that I could rid myself of by forgiving myself?
- Do I feel that I deserve to be forgiven?
- What difference would it make to me and others if I could forgive myself more?

KEY 5: NO REGRETS

The past does not have a future, but you do.
Byrd Beggett

Life is filled with choices. Some choices are good and others are not. We could have chosen differently and our lives would have been different. We all have regrets about the past, which is normal because we are human and make many mistakes and wrong choices over the course of our life. Some are more serious than others and may have a huge impact not only on our own life but on other people's lives.

Bronnie Ware from Australia wrote the book *The Top Five Regrets of Dying*[1]. She had nursed dying people and came to the conclusion that what they regretted most were the following:

1. I wish I'd had the courage to live a life true to myself, not the life others expected of me.
2. I wish I hadn't worked so hard.
3. I wish I'd had the courage to express my feelings.
4. I wish I had stayed in touch with my friends.
5. I wish I had let myself be happier.

Aren't all those regrets very sad? Here are some comments on each of them.

I wish I'd had the courage to live a life true to myself, not the life others expected of me. Is this regret more common among women than men? I think so, especially in women of my generation. Women have learnt to take care of others and think less of themselves, with the result that they sometimes act as a martyr.

Many men also live more or less according to what is expected of them by others. It may concern career, making money, having a house and a car that are similar to those of their neighbours. A price for building a career can be that they miss out on spending time with their family. In other words, they have the second regret *I wish I hadn't worked so hard.*

Is it too late to do something about these two regrets when you are middle-aged or already approaching retirement? Only if you believe it is. For example, many senior men I know spend a great deal of time taking care of their grandchildren, which they enjoy very much and it is a way of compensating for the lack of time they had with their own children. Is it too late to bond with your adult children? Why should it be? Good relationships with adult children can be very rewarding both for the children and their parents and I am sure you can help them in various ways. The same goes for the regret *I wish I had stayed in touch with my friends.* It is never too late as long as they and you are alive! It is never too late to find new friends either. But you may have to work at it.

The two regrets *I wish I'd had the courage to express my feelings* and *I wish I had let myself be happier* may be similar. If you have the courage to express your feelings your chances of being happier will increase. Is it too late? Not at all! In fact, many people discover that as they approach middle-age or grow older they have more courage to express their feelings than when they were younger. For various reasons they simply don't worry as much about what other people are thinking. If you make an effort to find out who you have become and who you would like to be you can also let yourself be happier now than you have ever been.

"Non, je ne regrette rien" (No I have no regrets) sang the famous French singer Edith Piaf. But what is regret and why is it important to learn more about it?

Regret means that we blame ourselves for a bad outcome, for a previous choice that we wish we could undo as it makes us sad thinking about how things might have been if we had made a different choice.

In an article called "The Psychology of Regret" Melanie Greenberg[2] asks if there is any value in regret and refers to the researcher Neal Roese, who stated that regret is of informational value, especially to younger people, as it can help them to make corrections. The function of regret is to help us make sense of the world, avoid negative behaviours, gain insight and improve our ability to achieve desired outcomes.

There is a saying that what we regret the most are those things we did not do, not what we did. Is it true? Do people experience regrets differently when they look back over long or short periods? The answer seems to be that people are more likely to regret actions taken and mistakes made over short time periods. On the other hand, over long time periods they are more likely to regret actions not taken.

As mentioned above, we can learn from our regrets, which is both very positive and meaningful. A reason to let go of your regret and self-blame is its negative effect on your health. According to Greenberg, regret can result in chronic stress and negatively affect our immune system. Regret impedes the ability to recover from stressful life events and extends emotional recovery.

Greenberg also mentions that there are differences between men and women and between different cultures in how people experience regret. Women have more difficulty disengaging from past relationships, while men have a tendency to replace lost relationships more quickly by finding new partners. The cultural differences concern how much control people have over their life choices. In cultures where individual choices are restricted and regarded as less important, people accept the situation more easily due to the lack of other choices.

Furthermore, Greenberg mentions that another strategy for coping with regret is to accept what cannot be changed. You may also have to forgive yourself and let it go. You can consider the circumstances at the time, as well as the fact that you did not have all the knowledge that you would have needed or have now.

The researchers Mike Morrison and Neal J. Roese[3] studied regrets of the typical American and presented the results in the article "Regrets of the Typical American: Findings From a Nationally Representative Sample". A total of 370 adult Americans completed a survey via the telephone. The result was that the biggest regret centred around love relationships, i.e., lost love and unfulfilling relationships, a divorce or other related decisions. Family was the second most regretted life domain, while the third was education. The study also showed that inaction regrets lasted longer than action regrets.

According to another study, "Life Regrets and the Need to Belong" by Mike Morrison, Kai Epstude and Neal J. Roese[4], there is a link between regret and the need to belong. The authors conclude that the findings highlight the central role played by social connectedness in what people regret most.

Another American study was carried out by Karl A. Pillemer[5], who found that when the 1,200 elders in his Legacy Project reflected on their lives they repeated over and over things such as "I would have spent less time worrying" and "I regret that I worried so much about everything". In these people's view worrying is a waste of precious and limited lifetime and worry is an unnecessary barrier to joy.

Here are some examples: John, 83, said: "Don't believe that worrying will solve or help anything. It won't. So stop it." A 102-year-old woman, Eleanor, said: "Well, I think that if you worry, and you worry a lot, you have to stop and say to yourself, 'This too will pass.' You just can't go on worrying all the time because it destroys you and your life, really…So the most important thing is to take one day at a time."

The interviewees also presented some pieces of advice:

Tip 1: Focus on the short rather than the long term.
Tip 2: Instead of worrying, prepare.
Tip 3: Acceptance is an antidote to worry.

Do you ever wish that you could live your life over again? Here is what a woman who lost her battle with cancer would have done differently.

If I Had My Life to Live Over
- I would have talked less and listened more.
- I would have invited friends over to dinner even if the carpet was stained and the sofa faded.
- I would have eaten the popcorn in the "good" living room and worried much less about the dirt when someone wanted to light a fire in the fireplace.
- I would have taken the time to listen to my grandfather ramble on about his youth.
- I would never have insisted the car windows be rolled up on a summer day because my hair had just been teased and sprayed.
- I would have burned the pink candle sculpted like a rose before it melted in storage.
- I would have sat on the lawn with my children and not worried about grass stains.
- I would have cried and laughed less while watching TV – and more while watching life.
- I would have shared more of the responsibility carried by my husband.
- I would have gone to bed when I was sick instead of pretending the earth would go into a holding pattern if I weren't there for the day.
- I would never have bought anything just because it was practical, wouldn't show soil or was guaranteed to last a lifetime.
- Instead of wishing away nine months of pregnancy, I'd have cherished every moment and realized that the wonderment growing inside me was the only chance in life to assist God in a miracle.
- When my kids kissed me impetuously, I would never have said, "Later. Now go get washed up for dinner."
- There would have been more "I love yous"…more "I'm sorrys"…
- But mostly, given another shot at life, I would seize every minute…look at it and really see it…live it…and never give it back.[6]

What regrets do you have? Did you recognize yourself in the above mentioned examples of regrets? I did, but only partly. I think it is important to remember that regrets may differ a great deal between individuals. We are not all the same! Our life experiences vary very much. In addition, there are cultural differences.

Maybe you regret that you did not have the courage to dare and take more risks.

Maybe you wish you had not taken life so seriously. Perhaps you regret that you did not have more fun or joy in your life. Maybe you wish you had been a more generous person or that you had been kinder to people whom you cared for.

When I think of the regrets I have, I realize that many of them have to do with me together with other people, people I have hurt by saying the wrong things or by not speaking to them when I should have. I blame myself for having expected too much, for example expecting a close friend to know or understand things she just could not know or understand. I blame myself for having been immature, which is really stupid! We aren't born mature, are we? We grow throughout our entire life and some of the things I blame myself for are just part of my experience and helped me to grow and mature!

I especially regret things I did or didn't say to people who were close and important to me but are now dead. For example, I regret arguments I had with my mother and how I wanted to prove I was right. I regret not having had the courage to admit when I was a child that I had broken or damaged something and others who were innocent were accused of having caused the damage.

It is sad to think about these regrets but what can we do about it now? Probably not much, except to forgive ourselves and others. The past is the past. We cannot change our history, so the best we can do is to focus on the good things that happened in life and be grateful for them. This will probably enable us to focus on the present to a greater degree. We can only control and influence the present. Living life one day at a time means living all the days of your life.

Sometimes we get a second chance or a second best time as expressed below:

The best time to plant a tree was 20 years ago. The second best time is now.
Chinese proverb

Leaving Behind and Moving on

The truth is that unless you let go, unless you forgive yourself, unless you forgive the situation, unless you realize that the situation is over, you cannot move forward.
Steve Maraboli

There are many situations in life when you are confronted by a need to leave behind and move on. It can happen when you lose your job, are going through a divorce, become physically disabled or financially ruined. When you retire you have to leave many things behind that have been important to you, such as work identity, title, status, power, colleagues, customers, clients and so on. You may also have to leave behind a certain structure of the day and year, learning opportunities, the feeling of belonging and of being useful and needed.

Furthermore, you will experience some personal losses that have nothing to do with your job, such as looking young, physical strength, a "limitless" future and the fact that a big part of your life has passed and is gone forever. You may have to make peace with your body as one of the informants in my survey mentioned.

To be able to feel joy, it is important to be aware that these losses exist and allow yourself to regret and miss them. Furthermore, it is vital to take time to adapt emotionally and practically to changed circumstances. But life does not stop because you grow older. It is just a new chapter that is about to start and it can be the best chapter of your whole life, if you allow it to be and make the right choices.

Most of us have difficulty moving on. We dwell in the past and focus on the mistakes we made. In order to move on you have to remind yourself that life is short and a journey, not a destination. Twenty years from now you may be disappointed about things you did not do today in the same way as you now regret what you did or did not do long ago.

What happened in the past happened. Don't deny it but try to understand it and the fact that you cannot change the past. Recognize that your past has contributed to who you are today. Search for the lessons of the past. You can respect and learn from your previous mistakes in order to avoid repeating them. Look at your life as a whole instead of dwelling on a few negative aspects. When you made the wrong choices they were based on the experiences and beliefs that you held at the time. You were being you.

As adults and even more so as seniors we have a range of experiences, some of which concern everyday life. You know how to handle things because you have learnt by experience. This implicit learning resulted in tacit knowledge. We also know a great deal about feelings. We are familiar with pain and have experienced happiness. We know that emotions are part of being human but we handle them in different ways. We cannot live our whole life without being hurt or hurting other people. We also have a choice in terms of our feelings. We can choose to feel sorry for ourselves or leave things behind. We can choose to blame ourselves or be a victim or decide to take control of our resentments, anger, or sense of not being worthy.

Gratitude and forgiveness may also help us to have fewer regrets and move forward.

Here is an exercise that may help you: Write a letter to your younger self when you were 25 or 40 years old about your present life. This letter may help you to see how far you have progressed, to let go of the past and stop you from focusing on your regrets. You will realize that you have overcome many difficulties in your life and progressed this far! Isn't that amazing?

Being curious and learning new skills may also help you to move on and leave the past behind. I will discuss that in greater detail in the following section.

Curiosity and Learning

Learn from yesterday, live for today, hope for tomorrow. The important thing is not to stop questioning.
Albert Einstein

Being curious and wanting to learn more is important if you wish to have more joy in your life irrespective of your age. If you lose your curiosity or never had much you risk stagnating and having a boring life.

When you're curious, you find lots of interesting things to do.
Walt Disney

There is a well-known saying that "you cannot teach an old dog new tricks." There are several good replies whenever you hear that saying. To me, one of the best is that we are not talking about dogs. We are talking about human beings, so what have dogs got to do with it?

On a more serious note, the biggest problem with that saying is that so many younger and older people believe it and therefore miss out on a myriad of opportunities. Another problem is that there are some seniors who prove that the saying is true. We probably all know some older people who have no idea how to use a smart phone, to shop online or even send e-mails. In their own view, they are too old to learn and are simply not interested. That is understandable, as information technology (IT) can be experienced as a big challenge, especially when we grow older. I know! But with the help of a little curiosity many would discover that learning to use some of the new technical devices is not that difficult and above all very useful and even fun. So please don't give up, because it is very rewarding to try keeping up with at least some technical challenges!

There are many stereotypes about IT and older people. However, there are large numbers of older people who are both very interested and extremely competent when it comes to IT. Some of them enjoy teaching and helping others and there are also many senior network associations with millions of members all over the world.

Robert Chen[7] writes that after learning a huge amount as young children, then at school and finally in working life, we come to a point where we are not obliged to learn anymore and it becomes optional. This is the point at which some people choose to stop learning new things and others continue to learn. Some use the excuse that they cannot learn new things because they are older and once they make this choice their ability to learn weakens in the same way as any unused muscle.

A conclusion is that if you want to be good at learning new things, it is important to keep learning.

Maybe you have your doubts. For example, couldn't it be too late to learn a new language? No, it isn't! I am example as I learnt Thai at the age of 66-70. I speak well enough to make myself understood and I am not talking about Thai for tourists. I can also read Thai fairly well. But you must be motivated and it may take a little longer to learn when you are older.

In my experience learning a new language as an adult is always hard work. You forget what you have learnt whether you are 20 or 70 years old. I know because I speak seven languages and most of them I struggled to learn when I was young. Much of what I learnt I forgot when I had too few opportunities to practice the language.

Stereotypes about seniors and learning languages are common as Jeff Anderson[8] points out:

> Traditional ideas about how we learn language say that older adults are poor second-language learners. This misconception is based on long-standing theories about language acquisition, and also outdated stereotyping of seniors.

Stereotypes about age are the biggest obstacle, as they make you believe that you are too old to try. In her article "Older Learners: Challenging the Myths" Alexandra Withnall[9] writes about other stereotypes as well, such as "Older people forget things and are too slow to learn anything new."

Many of us have experienced that we forget names or words or mislay objects, which sometimes starts in middle age. But unfortunately, this may translate into a misconception that the memories of older people are poorer than they are in reality and that they are unable to learn new skills or make use of new knowledge.

On the other hand, it is true that the mind becomes a little slower with age and a decline in memory starts when people are in their 20s or 30s. However, memory can improve with training in both younger and older people. Motivation is what matters when it comes to memory and learning.

Another misconception or myth is: "Older people live in the past and don't like changes." I think Alexandra Withnall is correct when she states that older people enjoy sharing their reminiscences about the past as a way of cementing relationships with others of the same generation. But this does not mean that they are not interested in the present!

Another myth that Alexandra Withnall writes about is: "Older people are not interested in learning." I hope you agree with me that this generalization is simply not true!

My doctoral thesis is entitled *Age and Work - Conceptions of the Significance of Age for Middle-Aged Employees*[10] and its main study consists of interviews with people aged 45-54. Generally, the interviewees were satisfied with being middle-aged. They maintained that it is people with stereotyped expectations of middle-aged individuals, not they themselves, who have a problem with their age. I think the same may also be true when it comes to retired people, as it is not them but the people around them who have an age problem.

There are other stereotypes about age and work. Older people are considered less productive than younger workers in spite of the fact that today we know that most individuals maintain their mental competence and learning abilities well into old age and have the advantage of a great deal of experience and tacit knowledge. In reality, many older people all over the world do work, although it is not always looked upon as a job when older women take care of parents, parents-in-law, partners or grandchildren. For example, in sub-Saharan Africa, 20% of rural women aged 60 and over are their grandchildren's main caregivers.[11]

Furthermore, whether you are middle-aged or senior you can attend courses and lectures of various kinds and enjoy it. You can learn practically anything you want as long as you are motivated, interested and curious.

When I was a senior lecturer for 12 years, the saying that one of the best ways to learn is to teach was confirmed. Of course the same is true whether or not you have retired. You can learn by being a mentor or by lecturing. You can teach by talking to others of all ages about your experiences and knowledge.

You can also teach as a teacher. A friend of mine who is 85 years old is a good example of that. She is a study circle leader for other seniors helping them to improve their French and Italian and she has been doing so for over 15 years. In this way she helps other seniors, but it is also a way for her to keep her own French and Italian up-to-date. In addition, she also helps immigrants to practice speaking Swedish under the auspices of the Red Cross. Talk about role models!

The illiterate of the 21st century will not be those who cannot read or write, but those who cannot learn, unlearn and relearn.
Alvin Toffler

Hope

Learn from yesterday, live for today, hope for tomorrow.
 Albert Einstein

Did you ever think about how much power there is in hope? According to a well-known proverb, hope is the last thing to be lost. When you carry hope in your heart, miracles can happen. I think we have all heard about situations that appeared hopeless but where there was life, there was hope and seemingly impossible goals were achieved.

Hope is about positive expectations and believing in the future. Being hopeful means that you want to do or achieve something that you believe might be possible, even when the situation is uncertain.

Hopefulness means saying to yourself that you won't give up, that you will keep on trying.

According to C.R. Snyder[12], hope has some ingredients: The first is goal-oriented thoughts. Goals should be challenging but attainable. Another ingredient is pathways to achievements. You must believe that there are one or more ways to achieve the goal. People with the highest levels of hope tend to generate multiple pathways. There must also be agency thoughts, meaning that you believe that you can both initiate and sustain the pathways.

You can use the past to help you find hope for the future. You have probably already experienced a time when things looked impossible and then turned out to be better than expected. You can try to recall a time in your past when something was actually going your way, only you did not know it then.

One of the wonderful things about hope is that it is contagious. Your hope can help other people find hope. You can also motivate other people to be hopeful by encouraging them to ask for help or to take one day at a time.

What else can you do to find hope in your own or other people's lives?

I attended a conference in India and had been listening to an interesting presentation called "Never too old for hope". Afterwards, there was time for questions and a young Indian woman took the microphone and told us a little about her life. She had lost her child, she was ill, she had no work and so on. "Where can I find hope?" she asked. Afterwards I spoke to her and mentioned the power of being grateful for what you have instead of focusing on what you don't have.

Later that day, I questioned whether I had done the right thing to talk to this woman about gratitude. What did I know about her and was it at all possible for me to understand her situation and suffering? I came to the conclusion that it was right to talk to her about gratitude. There are always things to be grateful for. I believe that focusing on what you hope for and have a reason to be grateful for instead of what you don't have can help you find the strength and means to improve your situation. I also believe that hope is connected to patience and means that you have to accept the uncertainty that is characteristic of a hopeful situation.

Here is a story about the power of hope.

Four Burning Candles
In a room there were four candles burning. The ambiance was so soft you could hear them talking.

The first one said "I am PEACE, however nobody can keep me lit. I believe I will go out." Its flame rapidly diminishes and goes out completely.

The second one says "I am FAITH. Most of all I am no longer indispensable, so it does not make any sense that I stay lit any longer." When it finished talking a breeze softly blew on it, putting it out.

Sadly, the third candle spoke in its turn. "I am LOVE. I have not got the strength to stay lit. People put me aside and don't understand my importance. They even forget to love those who are nearest to them." And waiting no longer it goes out.

Suddenly a child entered the room and saw three candles not burning. "Why are you not burning? You are supposed to stay lit till the end."

Saying this, the child began to cry. Then the fourth candle said, "Don't be afraid, while I am still burning we can re-light the other candles, I am HOPE."

With shining eyes, the child took the candle of Hope and lit the other candles.

The flame of Hope should never go out from our life so that each of us can maintain HOPE, FAITH, PEACE and LOVE.

Author Unknown[13]

KEY 6: LAUGHTER, SMILES AND HUMOUR

You may not be able to change a situation, but with humour you can change your attitude about it.
Allen Klein

Laughter

A day without laughter is a wasted day.
Charlie Chaplin

My ten year old granddaughter said to me: "Grandmother, you laugh too much!" My answer to her was: "But you know that laughing is my medicine. I have to take my medicine every day. Look at me, I take my medicine and I am very healthy!" She replied: "Yes, I know you are healthy, but your laughing is not the only reason!"

My granddaughter was right! Laughing is not the only reason why I am healthy but I think it is one of the reasons. Laughter both makes you feel good and is very beneficial to your health. Here are 10 benefits that laughter can bring:[1]

1. Protects the heart
2. Reduces physical aches and pains
3. Improves sleep
4. Reduces depression
5. Attracts others to us
6. Gives you an internal workout

7. Boosts the immune system
8. Improves alertness, creativity and memory
9. Relieves stress
10. Creates social connection

That is not bad, is it? In fact I find it amazing, so I intend to continue laughing every day! Maybe you are wondering what I do if there is nothing to laugh about. Some days are simply not that funny. But then I try to find something on TV, in a newspaper, on the Internet or in my memory just to get my medicine!

What about you? Do you laugh every day? In my opinion, you should! Let us take a closer look at the ten benefits of laughter. But before we do so, I would like to point out that behind such a general list of benefits are research results of various kinds and quality. As is often the case, more research may be necessary. Generally, studies have limitations. Examples are when studies are carried out with students as opposed to all age categories or based on exclusively male samples. Sometimes studies have small sample sizes and sometimes the results can be contradictory. We need to bear that in mind and you should also consider how the various benefits may apply in your case.

Having said that, I still believe that laughter is tremendously good for health so let us now take a closer look at the list of benefits.

1. *Your heart becomes stronger* and functions better when exercised. Laughter increases vascular blood flow and the functioning of blood vessels, which results in increased oxygenation of the blood. The risk of a heart attack is reduced.
2. *Laughter reduces physical pain and aches.* This has to do with the fact that endorphins are released in your brain. Research has revealed that when patients were told jokes after surgery and before painful medication they perceived less pain.
3. Scientific research confirms that laughter can help *improve our sleep patterns* by relaxing the mind and body.
4. *Laughter reduces depression.* As laughter triggers the release of endorphins it may help reduce depression.

5. *Laughter attracts other people to us* because people are attracted to laughter and good humour can keep relationships fresh and healthy.
6. A good belly laugh means that *your internal organs are having a workout or "internal jogging"*, especially your diaphragm, abdomen, respiratory and facial muscles and even your shoulders.
7. Research has shown that regular laughter *helps boost the immune system*, thus protecting against infections, the common cold and even cancer.
8. *Laughter improves alertness, creativity and has an impact on memory.* Laughter helps you remember what you have learnt.
9. *Laughter relieves stress* because certain stress hormones such as cortisone, dopamine and adrenaline are reduced by laughter and positive hormones such as endorphins and neurotransmitter levels are increased.
10. In addition, *laughter can connect us with other people*. Laughter is contagious and helps people bond. Laughter brings positive energy to other people, leading to more happiness and joyful relationships.

Has that information convinced you that my daily laughter medicine contributes to my health? Are you ready to try my prescription yourself? We were born with the gift of laughter, so it is a natural medicine. Laughter is not a learned behaviour, it is instinctual. People born blind and deaf still laugh.[2] We were all born with a chuckle muscle and it needs daily exercise.

For laughter to work as a medicine, how much and how often do you have to laugh? I do not think there is any correct answer to that question. You can laugh once or twenty times a day. The frequency is not important, nor how long you laugh. Just remember to laugh every day and if possible, enjoy a really good belly laugh now and then. The mere memory of it may make you feel good.

As I mentioned above, laughter is contagious. People can catch it from you and you can catch it from them. Sometimes we start laughing just because we hear somebody else laugh. Laughter has been described as "the shortest distance between two people."

What else can you do with laughter? You can laugh at yourself! That is a great idea, because if you laugh at yourself it means that you take yourself and your life less seriously. Can you laugh at your fears? Have a try! Laughing at yourself also reduces the risk of everybody else laughing at you!

To make mistakes is human; to stumble is commonplace; to be able to laugh at yourself is maturity.
William Arthur Ward

Laughter can also turn big problems into smaller ones. And in reality, aren't most of our problems small, if you look at them with humour? Think about it!

Sharing laughter adds joy to your and others' lives. You cannot feel anxious, angry or sad when you are laughing.

Faked laughter provides the same benefit as "real" laughter, because the body cannot distinguish between a faked and a real laugh. The positive physical effects are identical and faked laughter may lead to real laughter. Facial expressions alone create changes in your automatic nervous system.

Laughter makes you feel good and the feeling remains after you have stopped laughing. It also helps you to maintain a positive attitude when you encounter difficult situations, losses or disappointments. Laughter helps you to find hope and meaningfulness, to relax, recharge your batteries and keep things in perspective as well as increasing your quality of life, will to live and joy of life.

Our life circumstances are often beyond our control but we can control how we respond to them. Laughter is a socially acceptable outlet for pent-up emotions.

What happens when you laugh? Kathy Graham[3] refers to neuroscientist Sophie Scott, who stated that laughter involves breathing, emotions and the voice and is universal. People she studied who had no contact with the western world laughed in the same way. Babies laugh very early in their lives, in fact even before they are born. Not only humans laugh but also chimpanzees, gorillas, dogs and rats.

Elisabeth Walter[4] describes a study carried out by psychologist Jaak Panksepp, who specialized in studying the laughter of rats. He found that rats emit high-pitched chirps when tickled, playing with fellow rats and anticipating a reward. They also make the same sounds when they enter new environments or meet unfamiliar animals. Panksepp considers that this may be the same as nervous laughter in humans.

Rats, like humans, laugh less often with age. William Fry (referred to by Walter) found that kindergarteners laugh 300 times a day and adults only 17 times. But the rats who were tickled a lot when young usually retained the tendency to laugh later in life.

Maybe you should laugh more with children, grandchildren and other children in order to help them to be more prone to laughter as adults!

Smiles

Sometimes your joy is the source of your smile, but sometimes your smile can be the source of your joy.
Thich Naht Hanh

Not only laughter but also smiles are contagious. You will know that if you have been to Thailand, The Land of Smiles. If there is a confusion of tongues or confusion for other reasons it helps a great deal to smile. The smile is very useful!

A smile is difficult to give away because people tend to give it back. Smiling is a way of taking control of your emotions. You cannot feel unhappy when you choose to smile and it is difficult to frown when looking at someone who is smiling.

A smile has been described as a light on your face to let someone know that you are at home. Your smile will make the people around you more positive. Even when you do not feel like smiling and put a fake smile on your face you will start seeing your life in a more positive light and feel better, not only look happier. A smile can convey joy, warmth and compassion. Smiles are the beginning of laughter.

Christine Carter[5] suggests putting a pencil between your teeth horizontally, so that your smile muscles are activated. If you do that, you may find that your heart rate decreases and you start feeling calmer and happier. Smiling boots our immune system, reduces our stress level, lowers our blood pressure and makes people like us more.

Ron Gutman[6] has studied the power of the smile. He started by carrying out a longitudinal study that examined photos of students in an old yearbook. By measuring the smiles in the photos he could predict how successful they would become in future. Those who smiled the most had more fulfilling lives, longer lasting marriages, were generally happier and more inspiring to others.

In another study Gutman examined photos of baseball players and found that by looking at their smiles he could predict their lifespan. Players who did not smile lived for an average of 72.9 years, while players with beaming smiles lived for an average of 79.9 years.

Who smiles the most? Gutman refers to a study carried out by Dimberg, Thunberg and Grunedal and not surprisingly, the result was that children smile the most. They may smile 400 times a day whereas about 30% of adults smile more than 20 times a day and 14% less than five times a day.

According to Gutman, smiling makes us look good in the eyes of others and a study at Penn State University showed that we are even perceived as more competent when smiling.

Smiling stimulates our brain's reward mechanisms and H. Abel and R. Hester[7] state that smiling can reduce the level of stress hormones such as cortisol, adrenaline and dopamine, in addition to increasing the level of feel good hormones such as endorphins.

According to Paul Ekman[8], smiles are cross-cultural and have the same meaning in all societies. He distinguished between enjoyment and non-enjoyment smiles. Non-enjoyment smiles happen when the person smiles out of politeness or for other reasons that have nothing to do with her/his own enjoyment.

The difference between the two kinds of smiles is that in true enjoyment, for example when listening to a joke, not only the lips but also the outer part of the muscle that encircles the eye is activated. In most people this muscle does not obey the will and is only brought into play by a true and agreeable feeling, although a few people can voluntarily contract it. Those who frequently show smiles that involve the muscle around the eye also report feeling more happiness and being healthier.

If people don't smile at you, be generous and smile first. No man needs a smile more than the one who cannot smile himself.
The Dalai Lama

Humour

In matters of humor, what is appealing to one person is appalling to another.
Melvin Helitzer

Humour is said to be the fastest way to give as it can change pain into joy in a thousandth of a second. Humour can change a person's state of mind that quickly. With the help of humour you suddenly see the world in a different way. But in order to do that you have to be flexible and open to the fact that the world can be seen in a new light. Contacts are created with the help of humour and those who are good at using humour can help other people without becoming too emotional.

Humour helps you to stay emotionally healthier and shifts your perspectives so that you see situations in a more realistic way. When we laugh together we are united and become more spontaneous. Laughter unites people during difficult times and helps you to forget criticism and doubt.

Humour is subjective, which means that you and I may have very different views on what is funny and what is not. This has to do with the fact that there is a difference in each individual's unique perception. The perception of something as humorous also depends on many other factors, such as culture, maturity, geographical location and level of education. When we don't find a joke funny it may either be that it is offensive to us or that we just don't see the point because we do not have any knowledge of or emotional attachment to what the joke is about.

A study was carried out at the National University of Singapore by Ofra Nevo, Baruch Nevo and Janie Leong Siew Yin[9] in which 119 students of Chinese origin were asked to fill out questionnaires, state their favourite joke and describe a person with an outstanding sense of humour. The results were compared with those of the same studies in Israel and the United States. One of the findings was that the Singaporean students reported significantly less use of humour for coping. There were also differences in the kind of jokes they mentioned, in that the content of the jokes was less aggressive in Singapore compared to those provided by the American students. This is an interesting example of cultural differences.

Humour can also be therapeutic and here is a definition from the American Association for Applied Therapeutic Humor (AAHT)[10]:

> Therapeutic humor is any intervention that promotes health and wellness by stimulating a playful discovery, expression or appreciation of the absurdity or incongruity of life's situations. This intervention may enhance health or be used as a complementary treatment of illness to facilitate healing or coping, whether physical, emotional, cognitive, social, or spiritual.

Thus, humour can be dangerous to your illness!

Humour is also an educational tool that is useful not only in schools but everywhere in life. Humour stimulates both sides of the brain, so it can help you to grasp things more quickly and remember them for a longer time, understand more, as well as increasing your creativity and thought processes.

There are different kinds of humour, for example gallows humour and black humour, which are only used in specific circumstances. Gallows humour addresses serious, frightening or painful subject matter in a light or satirical way and is typically by or about the victim of such a situation, but not the perpetrator.

In black or dark humour, topics and events that are usually regarded as taboo, specifically those related to death, are treated in an unusually humorous or satirical manner while retaining their seriousness. The intent of black comedy, therefore, is often for the audience to experience both laughter and discomfort, sometimes simultaneously. Dark humour can help you in a stressful situation.

There are also sick jokes, which may be found in anecdotes intended to be humorous but are actually in very bad taste when they concern people who are handicapped in some way.

There are three main theories of humour: the incongruity theory, the superiority theory and the relief theory.

In the *incongruity theory* logic and familiarity are replaced by things that do not normally go together. We laugh at things that surprise us because they seem out of place. We expect one outcome and get another. We experience the incongruity between different parts of the joke as funny.

Here is an example of a joke based on the incongruity theory:

> Customer: Do you mind if I try on that dress in the window?
> Sales Assistant: Wouldn't it be better to use the fitting room?

According to *the superiority theory,* we laugh and look down at other people and their mistakes, stupidity or shortcomings. Below is a joke about a person who reveals her lack of knowledge of computers:

> Customer to the technical support: Good afternoon. I can't print. Every time I try, it says "Can't find printer." I've even lifted the printer and placed it in front of the monitor, but the computer still can't find it.

The relief theory is often used in films and plays to provide the viewers with a break when the tension is high. It is a theory about tension and release where laughter is supposed to release pent up energy.

Do younger and older people appreciate the same jokes? No. According to Nancy Recker[11], what people find funny seems to be significantly related to age. Young children, teenagers and adults laugh at different things. In his article "How laughter works" Marshall Brian[12] states that several obvious differences in people affect what they find humorous and that the most significant one seems to be age.

Another question is whether humour is always good for you. Again, the answer is no. As I mentioned above, not all kinds of humour are in good taste or worth laughing at. If you are a senior you can find humour and jokes about aging that usually highlight the negative aspects of growing old. This is quite common on birthday cards. In fact, such sick jokes can be quite humiliating for seniors and one can only wonder how younger people find them funny. Could it be that these jokes exist because of younger people's fear of aging?

Here are a couple of examples from birthday cards:

- May you unintentionally grow so old that you frighten small children.
- We can't wait until you have Alzheimer's so we can start re-gifting items to you from your own house.

Older people may also fear aging and want to keep their youthfulness. Here is a story about that, which also serves as an example of the incongruity theory, i.e., we expect one outcome and get another.

> A 90-year-old man was getting a pre-marital check-up and told his doctor he was preparing for his marriage to a beautiful 19-year-old girl. After an extensive exam the doctor shook his head and said to the man: "I am not sure this is such a good idea. It could prove fatal." The old man answered: "Well, if she dies, she dies."

So, what is considered funny can vary a great deal. It is important that you find out what is funny to you, so that humour can help you laugh and smile more and also to take yourself and others less seriously.

Ask yourself the following questions:

- When did I last laugh? What did I laugh at?
- What kind of humour do I like?
- What kind of humour do I not like?
- Do I surround myself with people who have a sense of humour?
- How can I help myself to laugh and smile more?

KEY 7: GOOD RELATIONSHIPS

Sometimes our light goes out but is blown again into flame by encounter with another human being. Each of us owes the deepest thanks to those who have rekindled this inner light.
Albert Schweizer

Having good relationships is important for many reasons. You can do things together, share interests, learn from each other, help each other and have fun together. Good relationships will make you feel that you belong and are appreciated, as well as being one of the most important keys to finding more joy of life.

During our working life many of our social relationship needs are met. We work together to achieve goals and spend time with other people at coffee breaks and lunch. Special occasions such as parties and birthdays, as well as our weekend and holiday memories are shared with our colleagues. We meet new colleagues, customers, patients, students etc.

When we retire, lose our job, move from one city or country to another or are going through a divorce we have the same need to belong to groups and have a social network. It is necessary to keep old friends and acquaintances but also to find new ones. You can become a member of an association, attend courses or participate in sports with people who share the same interests as you or try some activity or hobby that you never did before and find new people to socialize with. As a senior you can join pensioners' organizations or seniors' clubs to find other people of your age with the same interests, but don't forget to keep in touch with people of all ages.

Ways to Enhance Good Relationships

There are many ways to enhance good relationships, but you may have to start with yourself.

Do you blame others for what happens in your life, for what you feel or don't feel? Do you blame your parents, teachers, boss, or partner? If your answer is yes, it means you are giving power to other people. When you stop blaming others and start taking responsibility for your life you will feel much better! You are the captain of your ship. Observe and accept your own feelings, don't judge them, and do the same with other people's feelings.

Stop feeling sorry for people. It does not help them or you. Instead of feeling sorry you can start thinking positively and sending positive energy to the people you used to feel sorry for. In that way you can start helping them.

Do you criticize people who are different from you? You are not alone! But it is a fact that we are all different yet have the same basic needs. We all want to be loved and to love and be respected for who we are.

Do you always want to be right and find it difficult to accept the idea of being wrong? It is not possible to be right all the time and trying to be perfect is stressful and no fun for ourselves or others. Let go of being right about what is wrong with other people and their opinions.

The same goes for having to control everything that happens around you. If you could instead let go and allow the people around you to be just as they are you would feel much better and so would they.

Do you feel a need to impress other people? Stop trying to be someone you are not. Accept and embrace who you really are and you will discover that people are drawn to you.

People like you because of your personality and they want to socialize with individuals who give something back. People need to be respected and listened to. It does not mean that everybody's opinions are relevant for you. Choose whom you want to listen to and be influenced by.

Give up labeling or rejecting people or things just because you don't understand or know anything about them. Encourage other people to talk by repeating key words and phrases. That is a way of showing them that you want to understand what they are feeling and saying.

If you are worried about what other people will think stop trying to read their minds and instead ask them their opinion. Realize that others' truths are not your truths. What other people think about you is not fact, but mere words and thoughts. It says more about them than about you. Being concerned about what others think creates anxiety in you. You are doing your best, aren't you? Some people will like what you do and others won't. Brave people follow their hearts. Others follow other people's opinions.

Observe and listen to your own thoughts and self-talk. Don't believe everything that your mind tells you. Don't allow it to stop you! Remember that when someone acts in an inappropriate way towards you it may be caused by things that have nothing at all to do with you.

We easily forget how incredible we are. Don't allow others' truth to become your truth. Remember that through our own thoughts and actions we can do amazing things, which can help us soar. But if these things are termed deviant or different by others you may become discouraged because they don't seem to fit in with others' way of life. Words and thoughts from others are just noise, so get rid of them! Start listening to yourself instead.

Remember that there are many people out there who actually wish they could be even a fraction like you. Start believing in yourself and take advantage of how you can create a better life for yourself and those around you.

Be aware of the negativity around you. Who is negative and moans just for the sake of moaning? Make sure it is not you! How to handle negative people? You can try to turn the conversation in a positive direction. Sometimes it is best not to say anything or to walk away from the situation as soon as possible and keep your distance from that person. On other occasions the best thing to do is to tell the truth, that you would like to hear something positive and that you prefer people who can lift your mood instead of listening to meaningless moaning.

Surrounding yourself with positive people may be easier said than done. You cannot shut out people who depend on you or vice versa, such as family members, neighbours, colleagues etc. You have to be able to handle and accept many kinds of people who differ from you in their way of being or thinking and you can learn from them. Remember not to personalize somebody's negative attitudes. It probably isn't about you at all. On the other hand, you should avoid making excuses and accepting everything people say. Stick to your values and beliefs! Give others space but show them your boundaries. Avoid arguments with people when you know that their negativity can make you respond in the same way.

Not everybody is going to like you. Nor do you need them to like you. Allow yourself to find some people stupid or annoying. If you accept that it will be easier for you to accept that there are people who actually don't like you. Nobody can be loved by everybody.

There is a difference between being inspired and trying to copy other people. Allow yourself to feel the inspiration from people and look for role models.

Ask yourself:

- What are my three most significant relationships?
- How are they doing?
- What is one small thing I can do to make them feel better?
- Do I blame other people?
- Do I criticize people instead of encouraging them?
- Am I controlling in my relationships?
- Do I label people because they are different from me?
- Do I care too much about what other people will think or say?
- Do I surround myself with positive people?
- Have I found good ways to handle negative people?

Friendship and Kindness

Kind words can be short and easy to speak, but their echoes are truly endless.
Mother Teresa

Good friends can improve your mood, help you reach your goals by being encouraging, reduce your stress, support you through tough times and make you feel needed.

Do you believe that you cannot make new friends when you are middle-aged or a senior? That may be a limiting belief! You can find new friends but friends you have known for decades can never be replaced. You had better be patient with good friends you have known for a long time, accept that both they and you have changed and may have different wishes and goals for the future.

The best way to keep old friends and make new ones is to be a friend. When you want to meet new friends, remember that it is easier if you show that you are interested in them rather than trying to demonstrate how interesting you are. It also takes time to build close friendships.

Friendship is good for your health and friends may also be a wonderful support when life becomes difficult and illnesses and death appear. Friendship does not mean having the same view on things and sometimes a best friend can change your view on things or yourself. One of the cornerstones of friendship is loyalty.

Lawrence Robinson, Greg Boose and Jeanne Segal[1] describe what a friend is:

> A friend is someone who shares a deeper level of interaction or communication with you; he or she is someone you can really connect with, face-to-face. A friend is someone you feel comfortable sharing your feelings with, someone who'll listen to you without judging you or telling you how you should think or feel. As friendship works both ways, a friend is also someone

you feel comfortable supporting and accepting, and someone with whom you share a bond of trust and loyalty.

Friendship is about trust and here is a story about that.

The Bear and the Two Travellers
Two men were travelling together, when a Bear suddenly met them on their path. One of them climbed up quickly into a tree and concealed himself in the branches. The other, seeing that he must be attacked, fell flat on the ground, and when the Bear came up and felt him with his snout, and smelt him all over, he held his breath, and feigned the appearance of death as much as he could. The Bear soon left him, for it is said he will not touch a dead body. When he was quite gone, the other Traveller descended from the tree, and jocularly inquired of his friend what it was the Bear had whispered in his ear. "He gave me this advice," his companion replied. "Never travel with a friend who deserts you at the approach of danger."
Author unknown[2]

There is a difference between friends and acquaintances. An acquaintance is someone you exchange small talk with as you go about your daily activities or with whom you chat about sport. Acquaintances are important, but in a different way than friends.

Much of what is true about friends also applies to your partner. Probably she/he has also changed. You must allow each other to be the person you have become and would like to be. Each of you is a unique individual who can support and help the other to be and become the best and have joy in your lives.

Kindness makes for better relationships because when we are kind to each other we feel a connection. Especially in strained relationships you can experience how kindness can transform your connection.

When you are kind to others you inspire them to be kind. There will be a ripple effect. Kindness is contagious, brings positive side effects and also makes you feel joy. Here is a story about how a kind gesture can create a chain reaction:

One Gesture Can Create a Chain Reaction of Kindness
My friend and I were walking along the street chatting as a man was approaching from the opposite direction pushing a cabinet on a trolley. As we stopped to continue our conversation he stopped by his van, which was about 10 meters in front of where we were standing.

As he was elderly I asked him if he would like some help getting the cabinet into the back of his van. He replied with a smile thank you dear, I can manage. We carried on talking but I still kept an eye on him just in case. He did manage to get the cabinet into the van but it snagged on something and he was unable to get it all the way in so he went to the side door to try and pull it from there. At that moment my friend approached the van to help push it in and as she did that another stranger also went to help her and the gentlemen. It gave me the warm fuzzies, acts of kindness creating a chain reaction.

Here's an act of kindness that each and everyone of us can perform each day all day every day. Change your thoughts from sadness, anger, hatred, etc etc etc to thoughts of Happiness, Brightness and Love. Smile big and watch how your vibration will help change the world.
Brenda from Wellington, New Zealand[3]

Respect

Respect yourself and others will respect you.
Confucius

When you respect people you are kind and polite to them. We can always increase our level of politeness and courtesy. Respect also means accepting people, their way of being, as well as their values and experiences. When you respect yourself, others will sense it and respect you. I believe that is what Confucius meant in the above quotation. You can never have too much self-respect. It will also make it easier for you to respect other people. Listen to other people and try to understand them without attempting to change them. Be present and be patient.

If you want others to respect you, you have to respect them first. Respect is earned and not given. Gaining the respect of other people does not happen overnight. By respecting others you will find yourself respected. Treating and thinking about others as you wish to be treated and thought about is sometimes called the "Golden Rule". Trying to understand other persons' views means you show respect for their opinions. There is also a so-called "Platinum Rule", namely, how I treat myself trains others how to treat me.

A well respected individual is one who is honest in her/his communication and can be trusted to do what she/he promised. Be open to criticism. People respect someone who is able to accept negative feedback and turn it into something positive and who handles differences of opinions respectfully.

The word respect comes from the Latin word respectare, which means "to look once more" or "to see again". If you look beyond the first impression and your prejudices and take a deeper look, you will be more tolerant and realize that everybody has an absolute value. The contrary is when we are intolerant and assume that our own way of looking upon things and our own experiences are "right", the norm or the ideal.

When giving advice, do so with consideration. Show people that you understand their feelings and reasons without agreeing or analysing their problem from your perspective. To tolerate and respect other people you also need to be humble. People quickly forget what you said or did, but they never forget how you made them feel.

Being middle-aged or a senior you risk being looked upon by younger people as different, thus maybe not respected and taken seriously. But do you respect younger people? Do you accept them as they are, i.e., different from you and how you were at their age with other experiences and values? Listening to and respecting other people is important for your own personal development. Your views may be challenged, but this gives you a reason to reflect. By showing respect and being non-judgmental you increase your own self-confidence.

The meaning and significance of respect goes far back in history and can vary in different religions and cultures. For example, in the Bible the fourth of the Ten Commandments reads "Honour thy father and thy mother".

Another example is the meaning of paying respect in Thai culture and traditions. Showing respect for the Thai King and his family is not only polite, it's the law. There are special rules for how to pay your respect to Buddhist monks. Paying respect is also important in the daily life of Thai people. They pay respect by putting their hands together in a "waai" greeting that is actually a quite complicated way of greeting, thanking and paying respect with many rules to follow when it comes to how, who and when to waai.

Thai culture has its own very specific way of honouring older people. Showing respect to older friends and relatives is believed to be both a duty and the basis of good manners. The importance of a person's age makes it natural for Thai people to ask how old you are. Merely feeling and expressing respect for older people is not considered sufficient. Here are a few examples of how to pay older people respect in Thailand:[4]

You greet older people with a waai and speak in a quiet, respectful voice, using formal language. You never interrupt an older person and should never stand over or sit above her/him. Finally, the older person should be treated as an honoured guest, rather than a friend.

Other Asian cultures have similar ways of paying respect. For example, in Japan a bow is a highly regarded greeting that shows respect. Punctuality and avoiding touching people are other examples of ways to show respect.

Communication and Connection

The way we communicate with others and with ourselves ultimately determines the quality of our lives.
Anthony Robbins

Helping people and making a difference in their lives render our own life meaningful, which means that we feel a sense of belonging and connectedness. Here are a few quotations from my survey, where the informants describe what brings joy of life:

- *When I help people.* (Man, 70-79)
- *When I belong.* (Woman, 60-69)
- *When I feel appreciated.* (Woman, 70-79)

Helping other people makes us feel good and well. In order to help and connect with people you have to communicate. Start where you are. Talk to or smile at people you meet, even if you don't know them. Help a friend or neighbour. Compliment and praise people about something that is important to them. Express appreciation both to people you know well and people you don't know.

Not only what you say but also how you say it may be crucial. Being seen is a human need. Look at people when they talk to you, stop what you are doing and listen. When we fail to respond to people we care about we communicate messages such as "I don't see you, I don't hear you and you don't matter". This is also important when you talk to people without seeing them, for example on the phone. Doing other things, such as watching TV, reading a newspaper, eating and so on when talking to somebody on the phone is not respectful communication.

Long ago I learnt that listening is the most difficult part of communication, which I believe is true. I am also of the opinion that listening is the most powerful way to connect to other people. Listening is more important than understanding, because it means that you care. Does it ever happen that when you listen to somebody's story you interrupt the person and start telling about something similar that happened to you? This happens to me! In that way you shift the attention from the person to whom you are listening to yourself, which is not good communication! Instead you may hurt that person and it certainly shows a lack of respect.

Stay in touch with people. Show interest and concern if you want to have good relationships. We all know that we cannot take family and friends for granted. Many of us have already experienced several big losses in our lives when people close to us died. Do we act upon this knowledge? Yes, I think many of us do, but is it enough?

A positive word can have incredible power but it is amazing the damage you can do with a negative word. Be careful how you talk to people. Say what you mean and mean what you say. Be one of those special people who take the time to encourage. It will never be forgotten.

From the following story we can learn how powerful our words are. Discouraging words can kill and, while encouraging ones can save lives.

Two Frogs
A group of frogs was travelling through the woods, and two of them fell into a deep pit. When the other frogs saw how deep the pit was, they told the two frogs that they were as good as dead. The two frogs ignored the comments and tried to jump up out of the pit with all their might. The other frogs kept telling them to stop, that they were as good as dead. Finally, one of the frogs took heed to what the other frogs were saying and gave up. He fell down and died.

The other frog continued to jump as hard as he could. Once again, the crowd of frogs yelled at him to stop the pain and just die. He jumped even harder and finally made it out. When he got out, the other frogs said, "Did you not hear us?" The frog explained to them that he was deaf. He thought they were encouraging him the entire time.[5]

Do you feel alone and lonely? Many people of all ages do. You can feel alone and lonesome for many reasons. Being alone when that is not your choice may have a very negative impact on your joy of life.

Therefore, it is important to find various ways of connecting and gaining good company.

If you cannot meet people face to face as much as you would like, there are various ways of communicating, such as the telephone, e-mail, SMS, Skype, Facebook and other social media. Tell people how much you appreciate them, say thank you or offer them help.

Pets can be very helpful and useful as companions, as they reduce stress, provide the feeling of being needed and having something to care for.

Most of us probably think of a dog or a cat as a household pet but a goldfish, birds or a rabbit may be just as helpful. Laurence Robinson and Jeanne Seagal[6] highlight the physical and mental health benefits of pets. Here are some of the benefits:

- Pet owners are less likely to suffer from depression.
- People with pets often have lower blood pressure in stressful situations.
- Playing with a pet can elevate levels of serotonin and dopamine, which calm and relax.
- Pets may be good for your heart, pulse rate and muscles.

One of the reasons for the positive effect is that most pets fulfil the basic human need to touch. Pets can also help you to have a healthy lifestyle, for example by increasing exercise when taking a dog for a walk, providing companionship and someone to talk to, helping you to meet new people, adding structure and routine to your day and helping you find meaning and joy in your life.

An Australian study[7] revealed that 80% of dog owners talk to other people when out walking their dogs. A study of 89 Caucasian women whose spouse had recently died showed that for bonded dog owners, their dog could mitigate depression.[8]

Generosity

What we have done for ourselves dies with us. What we do for others and the world remains and is immortal.
Albert Pine

Generosity is a powerful tool for feeling joy, as well as for expressing love and appreciation. It is within your power and you are in control. Your self-confidence increases when you are generous and pleased with yourself. When you are generous you see yourself and others positively and your outlook changes.

Generosity can increase your joy of life and stop you from feeling lonely or depressed. Your life has a purpose when you decide to be generous, while giving to others helps you forget your own problems.

What can you give? Many things! You can of course give gifts or money. But you can also give other people emotional support. You can give them your time and attention. You can help them with things they cannot do themselves. You can share the experience and wisdom you have acquired. They can learn from you, you can help them grow and you can be a role model. At the same time you will learn and grow yourself.

You can be generous by accepting other people for what they are and allowing them to be who they are without trying to change or criticize them. Encouraging and inspiring other people is a way of changing the world. You can also encourage other people to be generous.

You can do many kinds of voluntary work. Perhaps you don't know what to start with. If that is the case just try anything and if you don't like it, try something else.

Jill Suttle and Jason Marsh[9] describe why giving may be good for you.

Giving makes us feel happy. It activates regions of the brain associated with pleasure, social connection and trust, creating a "warm glow" effect. Furthermore, *giving is good for our health.* Giving to others has been shown to increase health benefits in people with chronic illness. Older people who volunteered for two or more organizations were 44 percent less likely to die over a five-year period than non-volunteers. Similar results have been found among older couples who helped friends and relatives or gave support to their spouses.

Giving can promote cooperation and social connection. When you give to others your generosity is likely to be rewarded by others. When we give to others, we don't only make them feel closer to us; we also feel closer to them. *Giving evokes gratitude.* Cultivating gratitude in everyday life is a powerful key to increasing happiness and joy. Finally, *giving is contagious.* When one person behaves generously, it inspires observers to behave generously later, towards different people.

Here is a story from my life illustrating that you never know what may happen when you start giving.

Some years ago, a very generous person I knew died suddenly and too young. I wanted to do something that would make her death a little less meaningless. But what? Then one day, many months later, when I was going home from work by train, I noticed a small advert in a newspaper about children who needed sponsors. I knew immediately that I had found what I was looking for and that same evening I applied to sponsor a 4 year old girl in the east of Thailand. At the time I had never been to Thailand, but my granddaughter was also four years old and I thought that might be good!

Sponsoring that girl turned out to be one of the most rewarding experiences in my life and has affected so many people in a positive way. Now eight years later, I have visited her and her family four times, which meant enormously much to her, her family and to me. My financial aid means a great deal to them but also my being a role model and source of inspiration.

As I wanted to be able to say a few words in Thai to the little girl I had sponsored, I started to study Thai. Now many years later I am proud of being able to speak Thai well enough to make myself understood and also to read Thai, although it is the most difficult language I have ever tried to learn. It was not easy of course, and I both attended courses and studied with the help of private Thai teachers.

By visiting the girl I had sponsored and by studying the language I felt more and more at home in Thailand and a few years ago I bought a house there. I have written most of this book in Thailand, where I have found many new friends, both European and Thai.

What started due to a generous person's tragic death has turned a lot of people into winners; my Thai girl, her family, the people around them and not least myself.

What is stopping you from being generous? Could it be limiting beliefs? Could it be that you need to practice generosity more?

Could envy and jealousy be reasons? Some people envy their children, grandchildren or other children. What about you? Do you think that they are spoiled? When you were young, you did not get what children get now and they are not even grateful for what they have! But forget your envy! Be generous and happy for them that they have a more comfortable and stimulating childhood than you had. They will have their share of problems in life! You will be doing them a huge favour if you avoid telling them things that may result in limiting beliefs and low self-esteem. Instead, you can become their positive and generous role model.

You can also learn much more from children and young people if you have an open mind and try to see things from their perspective and they can learn so much from you, your wisdom, experiences and perspectives.

I remember a few years ago when my grandson was about four years old. He told me which computer games he liked the most. I said to him that I did not have any games on my computer. Not one! He looked at me as if it was hard for him to believe and then asked: "Not even when you were a child?"

Another reason for envy might be that other people have far more money than you have, so you envy them and may think it is unfair. Accept that life is unfair! Be happy for them and make the best of your own life and circumstances. There are still many choices for you to discover and make.

Thus, envy may be a hindrance in your life and it does not bring any joy to other people either. Look at the positive sides of your own life. Maybe you don't have what other people have. Perhaps you have things that they do not have. Look more at what you have instead of what you don't have.

What happens when you and your spouse or partner do not want to spend time or money in the same way? A generous attitude may help you to come up with solutions. Be happy for the other person's wishes and dreams. Leave the envy behind and be supportive instead. Want for others what they want for themselves.

Ask yourself the following questions:

- Am I as generous and giving as I would like to be?
- How can I become a more generous person?
- What can I give?
- To whom can I give?

Your Best Friend

Be your own best friend, not your own worst enemy.
Jerry Bruckner

A friend is a person who knows you well and loves you just the same. Who is your best friend? Could it be you? I believe having yourself as your best friend is the most wonderful thing you can achieve. You are the only person whom you cannot stop being together with. You spend more time with yourself than with any other person, so you might as well start liking yourself. Make yourself an interesting person to be with! You can do so by accessing the love and wisdom you have within you. Loving yourself as your best friend means that you embrace your whole being, the good and the less good. It is not other people's job to love you. It is yours!

Having yourself as your best friend brings joy into your life because it means that you will care for yourself as you would for your best friend, with the realization that you are not being selfish. Being your own best friend is necessary if you want to take care of others, as both you and they will benefit from your taking care of yourself.

Being your best friend, you will respect and appreciate yourself and be positive and grateful. You will focus more on what you have than on what you don't have. You will have compassion for yourself, be honest with yourself and forgive yourself in the same way as you would your best friend. This will increase your chances of being able to forgive other people.

If you are your own best friend you will treat yourself with generosity, kindness and speak in positive terms about yourself. Instead of being your own worst enemy, you can become your own cheerleader. It is your choice.

Being your best friend means that you will not be too hard on yourself and realize that you are good enough. You will accept your flaws and love yourself in spite of them. Being your best friend you will also have to make friends with your body. It might not be perfect but other people's bodies aren't perfect either.

You have already dealt with many challenges and overcome a host of difficulties. Whatever you are facing at the present moment, you should tell yourself as you would your best friend that you will overcome it. Being your best friend means that you will be able to take yourself less seriously and laugh at yourself and the things that happen to and around you. It could help you to change your perspective.

You will also allow yourself to ask for and accept help when needed. You will treat yourself with understanding when you experience a setback, which might help you get back on track again.

As your best friend you will allow yourself to feel and express emotions and permit yourself and others to be vulnerable. You will realize that being vulnerable does not mean that you are weak. On the contrary, it takes courage to allow yourself to be who you are, which reduces the stress of trying to be perfect. When you allow yourself to be vulnerable you also allow others to be vulnerable and to connect with you.

As your best friend you will remind yourself of the following quotation:

Be who you are and say what you feel, because those who mind don't matter and those who matter don't mind.
Bernhard M. Barush

Being your best friend and not your worst enemy you will put yourself first. That will bring more joy into your life and you may come to the conclusion that joy is the purpose of your life. With joy of life as your purpose you will see the colours in your life. You will go from a life of black and white to a life of full colour.

ACKNOWLEDGEMENTS

To me the Joy of Life is a powerful and beautiful concept and seems to be so for many other people as well. When I have answered the question as to what my book is about people have often said "Wow! That's interesting!" I agree! It is interesting! But what is also interesting is the importance of support when you are writing a book. You can't do without it!

I have been fortunate as there have been many people around me who have shown an interest in my book and willingness to help me in whatever way they could. However, not only people have been helpful and I would like to start by expressing my thanks to the Internet. Most of the book was written in Thailand, far from bookshops and libraries. Do you know how many interesting facts and articles you can find on the Internet? I can assure you that it is just incredible. You can be anywhere in the world and have access to so much knowledge!

However, by support I mainly mean people. I am so grateful for the support I received during the whole writing process. One of my very strongest supporters was Birgitta Qvarsell, professor emerita at the University of Stockholm. I admire your knowledge, your experience and way of guiding and encouraging me after reading my manuscript. The many long lunches we had together were invaluable and a great pleasure!

A great number of other people have read my manuscript at the beginning or at the end of the writing process or both. I would like to express my gratitude to the following people in Sweden: Anneli Liukko, PhD, who read the manuscript at an early stage. Kitty Gahnström Strandqvist, PhD, for reading my manuscript at the end of my writing process. Thank you for your valuable comments! I also thank Sara Silfverberg for reading and commenting on the whole manuscript. You were once one of my wonderful students. Sara, you are great!

I would also like to thank my Swedish friends Bo Talldal, Kurt Larsson and Marcus Karlsson for encouraging me and for interesting discussions about, among other things, the title of the book. I thank Ruby Mayeda in the US for believing in me and Tania Moloney in Australia for your constant support, encouragement and for being such a great friend!

I would like to thank the following people in Thailand: Nanna Islandi, my wonderful neighbour and friend, for reading my manuscript and for all our discussions about it. I also thank her husband Richard for support and very interesting discussions. I thank Gerd Hall for reading and providing me with valuable comments and Linnéa Brolin Holstein for reading, discussions and encouragement. Some people in Thailand have not read my manuscript but have supported me in other ways. Thank you Parinee Pedersen for your generosity and for sharing with me the joy of having finished my book. I also thank your husband Bjarne for reading the manuscript. Thank you Kun Thongphan for all our laughs. Many other neighbours in Thailand, both Thai and European, and friends in Sweden have been there for me in various ways. I thank you all!

Furthermore, I thank Eija Kuusela for her efforts and expert help with the beautiful book cover and Monique Federsel for proof reading my manuscript. I was so fortunate to find you Monique and so happy for your professional help!

I also thank my sons Anders and Erik and Erik's wife Karin together with my two grandchildren Isabel and Jesper for being the most important people in my life. I love you all!

NOTES

INTRODUCTION

1. Pattillo, Charlene Gaulle Story, Itano, Joanne. Laughter is the Best Medicine. *American Journal of Nursing.* April 2001, Vol. 101. Pp 4043. *Oncology Nursing Update 2001.* Retrieved on 16th November, 2013 from http://journals.lww.com/ajnonline/Citation/2001/0401/Laughter_is_the_Best_Medicine__And_it's_a_great.10.aspx.
2. Remen, Rachel Naomi, *Kitchen Table Wisdom.* Afterhours Inspirational Stories. Retrieved on 8th November 2014 from http://www.inspirationalstories.com/cgi-bin/printer.pl?58.
3. Carstensen, Laura L. Growing Old or Living Long: Take Your Pick. Retrieved on 3rd September 2014 from http:issues.org/23-2/carstensen/.
4. Attwood, Janet Bray, Attwood, Chris. (2008). *The Passion Test. The Effortless Path to Discovering Your Life Purpose.* New York: Penguin Group.

WHAT IS JOY OF LIFE?

1. Remen, Rachel Naomi, Embracing Life in *Living Life Fully.* Retrieved on 6th December, 2014 from http://www.livinglifefully.com/flo/flobeembracinglife.htm.
2. Selander, Ginger (2014). *Glädje i Vårdandets värld (Joy in the World of Caring)* Doctoral thesis, Åbo Akademis förlag, Åbo, Finland.

KEY 1: SELF-KNOWLEDGE

1. Branden, Nathaniel (1994). *The Six Pillars of Self-Esteem.* New York: Bantam Books.
2. Attwood, Janet Bray, Attwood, Chris. (2008). *The Passion Test. The Effortless Path to Discovering Your Life Purpose.* New York: Penguin Group.
3. Ibid.
4. Ibid.

5. Davenport, Barrie. You Find Your Passion But Lose Your Friends. Retrieved on 30th October, 2013 from http://www.bariedavenport.com.
6. Boyle, Patricia A, Barnes, Lisa L, Buchman, Aron W, Bennett, David A. Purpose in Life is Associated With Mortality Among Community-Dwelling Older Persons. *Psychosomatic Medicine* June 2009 Vol. 71 No. 5 574-579. Retrieved on 29th October, 2013 from http://journals.lww.com/psychosomaticmedicine/toc/2009/06000.
7. Steptoe, Andrew, Deaton, Angus & Stone, Arthur A. Subjective Wellbeing, health, and ageing. *The Lancet*. Early Online Publication. November 2014. Retrieved on 24th November, 2014 from http://www.thelancet.com/journals/lancet/article/PIIS0140-6736%2813%2961489-0/abstract.
8. The Parable of the Three Stonecutters. Retrieved on 13th November, 2013 from http://straighttogo.com/stonecutters/.

KEY 2: OPENNESS TO CHANGE

1. Weldon, Joel. The Sower's Seeds. Afterhours Inspirational Stories. Retrieved on 6th November, 2014 from http://www.inspirationalstories.com/1/165.html.
2. Empowering Articles Home. Retrieved on 4th November 2014 from http://yourbest13.homestead.com/.
3. A gift of inspiration. Retrieved on 5th October, 2013 from http://www.agiftofinspiration.com.au/stories/attitude/Touchstone.shtml.
4. Klein, Lauren. How Positive Emotions Improve Our Health. *In Greater Good. The Science of a Meaningful Life*, June 20, 2013, Retrieved on 15th October, 2013 from www.greatergood.berkely.edu/article/item/how_positive_emotions_improve_our_health.
5. Happiness Is A Choice. *Beliefnet, Inspire your everyday*. Retrieved on 20th October, 2013 from http://www.beliefnet.com/Inspiration/2003/01/Happiness-Is-A-Choice.aspx.
6. A gift of inspiration Retrieved on 30th October, 2014 from http://www.agiftofinspiration.com.au/stories/attitude/Attitude.shtml.

7. Attitude Determines Attitude. Retrieved on 2nd December, 2014 from http://www.motivateus.com/stories/altitude.htm.
8. Smith, Melinda, Segal, Robert & Segal, Jeanne. How to Stop Worrying. *Helpguide.org.* Retrieved on 15th October, 2013 from http://www.helpguide.rog//mental/anxiety_self_help.htm.
9. Walt Disney Quote. Think, Believe, Dream and Dare. *Larry Rivera's Space on the Web,* Retrieved on 11th November, 2014 from http://larryrivera.com/my-rants/walt-disney-quote-thinkbelievedreamdare/

KEY 3: GRATITUDE

1. Emmons, Robert A. Why Gratitude is good. *Greater Good. The Science of a Meaningful Life*, November 16, 2010. Retrieved on 10th October, 2013 from www.greatergood.berkely.edu/article/item/why_gratituded_is_good.
2. Emmons, Robert A. (2008). *Thanks! How Practicing Gratitude Can Make You Happier.* New York: Houghton Mifflin Company.
3. Emmons, Robert A. How Gratitude Can Help You Through Hard Times. *Greater Good. The Science of a Meaningful Life*, November 16, 2010. Retrieved on 10th October, 2013 from www.greatergood.berkely.edu/article/item/how_gratituded_can_help_you_through_hard_times.
4. Emmons, Robert A. 10 Ways to Become More Grateful. *Greater Good. The Science of a Meaningful Life*, November 17, 2010. Retrieved on 10th October, 2013 from www.greater-good.berkely.edu/article/item/ten_ways_to_become_more_grateful.
5. Afterhours Inspirational Stories. Retrieved on 3rd December, 2014 from http://www.inspirationalstories.com/10/1005.html
6. Gordon, Amie M. Five Ways Giving Thanks Can Backfire. *Greater Good. The Science of a Meaningful Life*, April 29, 2013. Retrieved on 10th October, 2013 from www.greater-good.berkely.edu/article/item/five_ways_giving_thanks_can_backfire.
7. Sand and Stone. Retrieved on 3rd December, 2014 from http://www.naute.com/stories/sand.html.

8. Emmons, Robert A. Pay it Forward. *Greater Good. The Science of a Meaningful Life,* June 1, 2007. Retrieved on 11th Nov., 2013 from www.greatergood.berkely.edu/article/item/pay_it_forward.
9. Academic Tips. Retrieved on 4th December, 2014 from http://academictips.org/blogs/a-glass-of-milk-paid-in-full/.
10. Emmons, Robert A. Pay it Forward. *Greater Good. The Science of a Meaningful Life,* June 1, 2007. Retrieved on 11th November, 2013 from www.greatergood.berkely.edu/article/item/pay_it_forward.
11. Maxwell, Victoria. Harness Gratitude in 9 Steps to Feel Less Lousy. Crazy for Life. In *Psychology Today* November 21, 1012. Retrieved on 8th November, 2013 from http://www.psychologytoday.com/blog/crazy-life/201211/harness-gratitude-in-9-steps-feel-less-lousy.
12. Jyotsna Collection of Short Stories Retrieved on the 12th November 2014 from http://jyotsnacollectionofshort-stories.blogspot.com/search?updated-max=2010-12-16T12:37:00%2B05:30&max-results=7

KEY 4: FORGIVENESS

1. Cohen, Adam. Research on the Science of Forgiveness: An Annotated Bibliography. Summaries of research on forgiveness, peace, and well-being. *Greater Good. The Science of a Meaningful Life.* Retrieved on 11th October, 2013 from http://greatergood.berkeley.edu/article/item/the_science_of_forgiveness_an_annotatedbibliography.
2. Luskin, Fred. The Choice to forgive. *Greater Good. The Science of a Meaningful Life.* Retrieved on 16th October, 2014 from http://greatergood.berkeley.edu/article/item/the_choice_to_forgive.
3. Luskin, Fred. Nine steps to Forgiveness. *Greater Good, The Science of a Meaningful Life.* Retrieved on 17th October, 2014 from http://greatergood.berkeley.edu/article/item/nine_steps_to_forgiveness.
4. Luskin, Fred. What is Forgiveness? *Greater Good, The Science of a Meaningful Life.* Retrieved on 13th October, 2014 from http://greatergood.berkeley.edu/article/item/what_is_forgiveness.

5. Kornfield, Jack. The Ancient Heart of Forgiveness. *Greater Good. The Science of a Meaningful Life,* August 23, 2011. Retrieved on 11th October, 2013 from www.greatergood.berkely.edu/article/item/the_ancient_heart_to_forgiveness.
6. Choquette, Sonia. (2009).The Power Of Forgiveness. Guest Article in *Chris Cade Liberate your Life*. Retrieved on 19th October, 2013 from http://www.chriscade.com/2009/10/the-power-of-forgiveness-by-sonia-choquette/.
7. Luskin, Fred. Nine Steps to Forgiveness. *Greater Good. The Science of a Meaningful Life*. Retrieved on 17th October, 2014 from http://greatergood.berkeley.edu/article/item/nine_steps_to_forgiveness.
8. Toussaint, Loren & Jon. R. Webb. (2005) Theoretical and Empirical Connections Between Forgiveness, Mental Health, and Well-Being. In Worthington, Everet, L. (Ed.) *Handbook of Forgiveness.* NewYork: Routledge, pp 349-362.
9. Cohen, Adam. Research on the Science of Forgiveness: An Annotated Bibliography. Summaries of research on forgiveness, peace, and well-being. *Greater Good. The Science of a Meaningful Life.* Retrieved on 11th October, 2013 from http://greatergood.berkeley.edu/article/item/the_science_of_forgiveness_an_annotatedbibliography.
10. Marsh, Jason. Is Anything Forgivable? *Greater Good, The Science of a Meaningful Life.*Retrieved on 13th October, 2014 from http://greatergood.berkeley.edu/article/item/is_anything_unforgivable.
11. Lazare, Aron. (2004). *On Apology,* Oxford: Oxford University Press.
12. Toussaint, Loren. & Webb, Jon R. Gender Differences in the Relationship Between Empathy and Forgiveness. *The Journal of Social Psychology,* 2003, 143 (6), p 673.
13. Lazare, Aron. (2004). *On Apology.* Oxford: Oxford University Press, p 23.

14. Breines, Juliana. The Healthy Way to Forgive Yourself. *Greater Good. The Secret of a Meaningful Life,* August 2, 2012. Retrieved on 11th October, 2013 from www.greatergood.berkely.edu/article/item/the_healthy_way_to_forgive_yourself.

KEY 5: NO REGRETS

1. Ware, Bronnie. (2012). *The Top Five Regrets of Dying.* A Life Transformed by the Dearly Departing. Hay House, Australia.
2. Greenberg, Melanie. The Psychology of Regret. *The Mindful Self-Express,* May 16, 2012. Retrieved on 19th November, 2013 from http://www.psychologytoday.com/blog/the-mindful-self-express/201205/the-psychology-regret.
3. Morrison, Mike & Roese, Neal J. Regrets of the Typical American: Findings From a Nationally Representative Sample. *Social Psychological and Personality Science,* 2011, online-version retrieved on 19th November 2013 from http:spp.sagepub.com/content 2/6/576.
4. Morrison, Mike, Epstude, Kai & Roese, Neal J. (2012). Life Regrets and the Need to Belong. *Social Psychological and Personality Science*, 2012, online-version retrieved on 19th November, 2013 from http:spp.sagepub.com/content/early/2012/02/01/19485506 11435 137.5
5. Pillemer, Karl. A. The Most Surprising Regret Of The Very Old – And How You Can Avoid It. HuffPost 50, November 18, 2013. Retrieved on 19th November, 2013 from http://www.huffingtonpost.com/karl-a-pillemer-phd/how-to-stop-worrying-reduce-stress_b_2989589.html.
6. Inspirational Stories. In Memory of Erma Bombeck. Retrieved on 3rd December 2014 from http://academictips.org/blogs/if-i-had-my-life-to-live-over/.
7. Chen, Robert. Why Old People Have a Hard Time Learning New Things. *Embrace Possibility Blog* retrieved on 23rd October, 2013 from http://www.embracepossibility.com/blog/why-old-people-have-a-hard-time-learning-new-things/.

8. Anderson, Jeff. Expanding Horizons: New Languages for the Elderly. *A Place for Mom,* May 25, 2012. Retrieved on 23rd November, 2013 from http://www.aplaceformom.com/blog/new-languages-for-the-elderly/.
9. Withnall, Alexandra. Older Learners: Challenging the Myths. Seminar/workshop 01 August 2005. Retrieved on 23rd October, 2013 from http://ler.letras.up.pt/uploads/ficheiros/8517.pdf.
10. Johansson, Ingrid. (1997). *Ålder och arbete. Föreställningar om ålderns betydelse för medelålders tjänstemän (Age and Work. Conceptions of the Significance of Age for Middle-Aged Employees.*) Doctoral thesis, Stockholm University.
11. Are you ready? What do you need to know about ageing? *WHO.* Retrieved on 22nd November, 2013 from http://www.who.int/world-health-day/2012/toolkit/background/en.
12. Snyder, C.R. (2000) *Handbook of hope: Theory, measures, and applications.* New York: Academic Press.
13. Inspirational Stories. Retrieved on 3rd December, 2014 from http://academictips.org/blogs/four-burning-candles/.

KEY 6: LAUGHTER, SMILES AND HUMOR

1. Barak, Edan, 10 Benefits Of Laughter in TOP10ZEN. Retrieved on 29th October, 2013 from http://www.top10zen.com/list/10_benefits_of_laughter-136?page=3.
2. Recker, Nancy. (2007). *Laughter Is Really Good Medicine.* Fact Sheet. Family and Consumer Sciences, The Ohio State University. Retrieved on 14th November, 2013 from http://ohioline.osu.edu/hyg-fact/5000/pdf/Laughter_Good_Medicine.pdf.
3. Graham, Kathy. *The Newsletter Think & Be Happy/* 3 May 2012. Retrieved on 19th October, 2013 from http://wellbeingaustralia.com.au/wba/think-and-be-happy-newsletter.
4. Walter, Elisabeth. Tickled Pink: Why Scientists Want to Make Rats Laugh. *Greater Good. The Science of a Meaningful Life,* Summer 2008. Retrieved on 11th October, 2013 from http://www.greatergood.berkely.edu/article/item/tickled_pink_why_scientists_want_to_make_rats_laugh.

5. Carter, Christine. Fake it Till You Make it. *Greater Good. The Science of a Meaningful Life,* February 17, 2009. Retrieved on 13th November, 2013 from http://www.greatergood.berkely.edu/raising_happiness/post/fake_it_till_you_make_it.
6. Gutman, Ron. The Untapped Powers of the Smile. Retrieved on 19th October, 2013 from http://blog.healthtap.com/2011/05/the-untapped-power-of-smiling/.
7. Abel, H. & Hester, R. (2002). The Therapeutic Effects of Smiling. *An Empirical Reflection on the Smile*, New York: Mellen Press.
8. Ekman, Paul (2003). *Emotions revealed. Recognizing Faces and Feelings to Improve Communication and Emotional Life*. New York: St. Martin's Griffin.
9. Nevo, Ofra, Nevo, Baruch & Leong Siew Yin, Janie. Singaporean Humor: A Cross-Cultural, Cross-Gender Comparison. Abstract. *The Journal of General Psychology,* Volume 128, Issue 2, 2001, pp 143-156. Retrieved on 21st November, 2013 from http://www.tandfonline.com/doi/abs/10.1080/00221300109598904.
10. The American Association for Applied and Therapeutic Humor (AATH). Retrieved on 24th October, 2014 from http://www.aath.org/generalinformation.
11. Recker, Nancy. (2007). *Laughter Is Really Good Medicine.* Fact Sheet. Family and Consumer Sciences, The Ohio State University. Retrieved on 14th November, 2013 from http://ohioline.osu.edu/hyg-fact/5000/pdf/Laughter_Good_Medicine.pdf.
12. Brain, Marshall. How Laughter Works. How Stuff Works. Retrieved on 21st November, 2013 from http://science.howstuffworks.com/life/laughter6.htm.

KEY 7: GOOD RELATIONSHIPS

1. Robinson, Lawrence, Boose, Greg & Segal Jeanne. How to make friends. June 2013 in *Helpguide.org.* Retrieved on 17th October, 2013 from http://www.helpguide.org/mental/how-to-make-friends.htm.
2. Afterhours Inspirational Stories. Retrieved on 13th November 2014 from http://www.inspirationalstories.com/2/237.html.

3. The Random Act of Kindness. Retrieved on 16th November, 2014 from http://www.randomactsofkindness.org/kindnessstories/3131-one-gesture-can-create-a-chain-reaction-of-kindness.
4. Thai Culture and Respect for Elders/Respect for Elders in Thailand, April 23, 2012. Retrieved on 13th November, 2013 from http://www.thailand-family-law-center.com/respect-thy-elders/.
5. Practical Success Secrets. Retrieved on 19th November, 2014 from http://www.practical-success-secrets.com/two_frogs.html.
6. Robinson, Laurance & Seagal, Jeanne. The Therapeutic Benefits of Pets, July 2013 in *Helpguide.org*. Retrieved on 27th October, 2013 from http://www.helpguide.org/life/pets.htm on 20131027.
7. Mishra, Vyvyan & Schröder, Bonnie. Measuring the Benefits. Companion Animals and the Health of Older Persons. Report. International Federation on Ageing, Global connection. Retrieved on 20th September, 2014 from ifa.v.org.
8. Bolin, Sharon, E. (1987).The Effects of Companion Animals During Conjugal Bereavement. *Anthrozoos: A Multidisciplinary Journal of the Interactions of People & Animals.* Vol. 1, No. 1, 1987, pp. 26-35. Bloomsbury Journals.
9. Suttle, Jill & Marsh, Jason. 5 Ways Giving is Good for You. *Greater Good. The Science of a Meaningful Life*, December 17, 2010. Retrieved on 18th October, 2013 from www.greater,good.berkely.edu/article/item/5_ways_giving_is_good_for_you

Printed in Great Britain
by Amazon